DEVELOPING
LEARNING
MATERIALS

Jacqui Gough

Jacqui Gough (AMIPD) is an experienced trainer and consultant and runs her own company, Flexible Learning Solutions (FLS), which specialises in providing, delivering, and producing open and flexible learning materials and courses. She acts as a consultant to companies in both the private and public sectors.

In the TRAINING ESSENTIALS series leading experts focus on the key issues in contemporary training. The books are thoroughly comprehensive, setting out the theoretical background while also providing practical guidance to meet the 'hands-on' needs of training practitioners. They are essential reading for trainers and for students working towards training qualifications – N/SVQs, and Diploma and Certificate courses in Training and Development.

Other titles in the series include:

Cultivating Self-development David Megginson and Vivien Whitaker

Delivering Training Suzy Siddons

Designing Training Alison Hardingham

Evaluating Training Peter Bramley

Identifying Training Needs Tom Boydell and Malcolm Leary

Introduction to Training Penny Hackett

The Institute of Personnel and Development is the leading publisher of books and reports for personnel and training professionals and students and for all those concerned with the effective management and development of people at work. For full details of all our titles please telephone the Publishing Department on 0181 263 3387.

TRAINING ESSENTIALS

DEVELOPING
LEARNING
MATERIALS

Jacqui Gough

INSTITUTE OF PERSONNEL AND DEVELOPMENT

First published in 1996
Reprinted 1998

Design and typesetting by Paperweight
Printed in Great Britain by
The Cromwell Press, Trowbridge, Wiltshire

British Library Cataloguing in Publication Data
A catalogue record for this book is available from the
British Library

ISBN
0-85292-639-1

**INSTITUTE OF PERSONNEL
AND DEVELOPMENT**

IPD House, Camp Road, London SW19 4UX
Tel.: 0181 971 9000   Fax: 0181 263 3333
Registered office as above. Registered Charity No. 1038333.
A company limited by guarantee. Registered in England No. 2931892.

Contents

Acknowledgements   vii

Introduction   viii

1 Planning Your Materials   1

2 Developing Your Materials   23

3 Guidelines on Graphic Design
     and Printing   42

4 Introduction to Open Learning   57

5 Technology-based Training (TBT)   76

6 Materials for Group and
     Individual Learning   110

7 Visual Aids   137

References   146

Index   148

Dedication
This book is dedicated to my husband, Peter

Acknowledgements

Many people have helped me in the preparation of this book. In particular, I would like to thank my husband, Peter, for his support and encouragement while I wrote this book.

This package contains a number of examples/screen shots that are Crown Copyright materials, originally published in training packages developed by Simulation Training, The Open College, and Xebec. They are reproduced here with their kind permission.

I would also like to acknowledge contributions from the following individuals and organisations, and thank them for the information and time they so generously gave: Nicola Staveley, MLS, Peritas, Simulation Training, Solent Video, The Team Talk Partnership, The National Extension College, The Open College, and Xebec for their kind permission to use quotations.

I Introduction

Learning materials come in many forms – role-plays, case-studies, handouts, videos, audio, text-based open learning, technology-based training, and others. All play their part in ensuring that training sessions are enjoyable, participative, meaningful, and, most importantly, meet their objectives.

To be successful, materials need to be structured, succinctly written and developed in formats designed for the purpose. Inappropriate and badly designed learning materials lead to ineffective training and learner dissatisfaction.

This book addresses these issues, and suggests ways you can create interesting and creative materials which appeal to the audience and meet your needs.

The book is split into seven chapters. Chapters 1–3 provide guidelines on how to plan, develop, and present learning materials. Chapters 4–7 build on the guidelines. The aim is not to provide a comprehensive book on how to develop *all* learning materials – many of them justify books in their own right. This book is intended as a guide to developing some of the most commonly used materials by trainers in conventional training sessions and open learning (namely, text-based open learning and technology-based training materials).

For the designer, this book will help you to select appropriate materials, find creative design solutions, and (I hope) encourage you to explore some of these areas further.

1

Planning Your Materials

Introduction

Whatever type of materials you are developing – text-based open learning materials, TBT (technology-based training), materials for group learning, or other training events – planning is a key part of the process. In order to plan well, the designer of training materials needs to focus on what is to be achieved if he or she is to be assured of success. The designer needs to develop a *design specification* (sometimes known as the *training specification*), on which agreement should be reached before detailed design work commences.

In this chapter I discuss how to select appropriate training materials in order to arrive at a design specification.

How people learn

First, it is essential to understand how people learn. We need to look at the learning cycle and at learning styles. (For a more detailed discussion, see Alison Hardingham's book in this series, *Designing Training*, London, IPD, 1996.)

The learning cycle

We are primarily interested in learning based on experience – 'experiential learning'. This means acquiring new knowledge or ways of behaving that will help you to do or see things differently; it can be viewed as a circular process known as the 'learning cycle'. In his work David Kolb has identified four stages in the learning cycle: experience, reflecting, theorising, and experimentation (see Figure 1).

Figure 1

THE LEARNING CYCLE

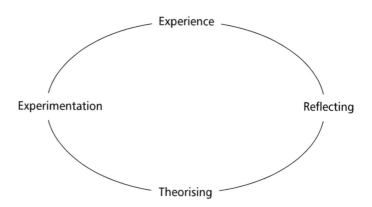

Learning is very much part of everyone's life, something that is happening all the time wherever we are. In business, people learn from one another and from their own experiences, eg by adapting to meet change. Many people believe that they learn best from their own experience rather than by being taught. The workplace can provide many 'learning opportunities' to help individuals develop.

Learning styles

People have preferences for the way they learn. For example, some prefer to learn by observing and reflecting rather than by doing and experiencing. These preferences are known as a person's learning style. In their book *The Manual of Learning Styles* Peter Honey and Alan Mumford have identified four learning styles; these correspond broadly to the four stages of the learning cycle.

Table 1

LEARNING STYLES

Category	How they learn
Activist	by doing and experiencing
Reflector	by observing and reflecting
Theorist	by understanding the reasons behind things – eg concepts and relationships
Pragmatist	by active experimentation, 'having a go', to see the practical application of what is being learnt

Although people have a preferred learning style, in practice they often draw on a mixture of styles. (For instance, someone may have two preferred styles, eg activist and reflector.) A preference for one or more styles indicates when a learner is likely to make sense of what is being learnt. It also indicates at which point in the learning cycle he or she is most likely to enter. The designer should keep these differences in mind when developing materials to ensure they are suitable for the person and the situation.

The development process

The development process for learning materials is a sequence of activities such as those in Figure 2 on page 4. In practice, though, some of these activities may run parallel.

The process outlined in Figure 2 may seem too structured an approach, but I find that, considering the amount of time it saves, it is worth the effort in the long run. It provides me with a clear focus on what I am trying to achieve. If a structured approach is not followed, the quality of the result tends to suffer.

Figure 2

A FRAMEWORK FOR GETTING THINGS DONE

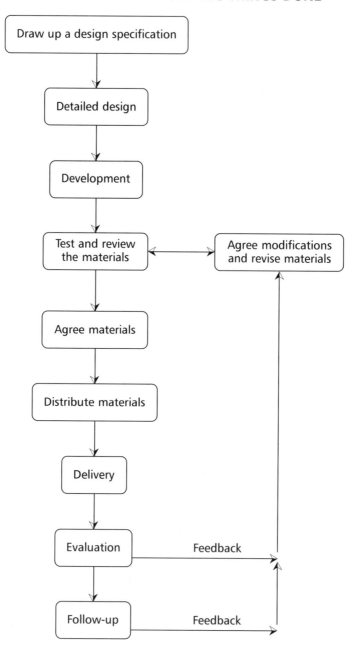

The design specification

A typical design specification looks at the general shape and sequence of the activities that make up the learning materials. Considerations at this stage should include:

■ the scope of the training event
■ the organisation's expectations of the proposed training – the desired outcomes
■ the standards and competencies required
■ a 'profile' of the learners
■ objectives
■ outline content
■ appropriate training methods
■ resources, time-scales, costs, and support
■ details of the learning environment.

The time it takes to complete the specification depends, of course, on the complexity of your materials.

Identifying the learning needs

Identifying the learning needs is crucial to the development of effective materials. There are various ways to do this, ranging from a full-blown survey to simply talking to the relevant managers or directly to the learners themselves. (A useful reference source on this topic is Tom Boydell and Malcolm Leary's book in this series, *Identifying Training Needs*, London, IPD, 1996.)

Experience shows that it is important to gain commitment from *all* those whose support you will need (including senior managers). Involving key people in this process from the start not only ensures that relevant and up-to-date information is gathered but also helps you to gain commitment to the training activity, thereby ensuring its success. With large projects you may want to consider a team approach to development: this can give people a feeling of ownership, and it also helps to gain their commitment. A few other ways I have used to gain commitment are to involve people at the planning stage (in order to identify needs and objectives), and to keep key people informed about developments, either formally or informally.

The scope of the training event

You need to make a clear statement of what you are trying to achieve, ie to set limits within which you can design and develop your materials. Exactly how you describe the scope of your training event depends on the task in hand. You may be developing materials for:

- a complete training programme
- a training course to meet the needs of a particular department (eg a new accounting system)
- training for a specific job (eg superviser, operator) or skills (eg customer care, how to operate a piece of equipment).

For example, let us say that a retail company that has introduced a new accounting system wants to develop a programme to train their staff in its use. The scope of the training event might be:

> To develop positive attitudes to the new accounting system among staff and management, and to ensure that they have the skills to operate it effectively.

Performance standards and competencies

The purpose of training and development is to enable individuals to perform activities to a required standard in order to meet objectives. Standards can be set at organisational, departmental, team, or individual level – and any one level may affect the others. For example, organisational objectives affect departmental objectives, which in turn affect the team's, and individual, objectives. How an individual performs is linked to the success of the other three levels in meeting *their* objectives.

The designer needs to identify clearly what the desired

outcomes of the training event are:

▮ What do people need to be able to do?
▮ What needs to be achieved as a result of their improved performance (ie 'the outputs')?
▮ How well do the tasks need to be performed in order for the objectives to be met?

Establishing the standards of performance and the competencies that you want the learners to achieve as a result of training enables you to set clear and measurable objectives. I have found that such standards are useful for a number of purposes: to identify areas for development (eg by managers and their staff); as a check-list against which learners can assess both themselves and others; as an aid towards assessing the competence of individuals; and for assessing the effectiveness of training.

Two useful sources for identifying standards are internally agreed standards and competencies specific to your organisation, and relevant NVQ (national vocational qualification) standards for the profession. The introduction of NVQs has meant that training needs are easier to identify, and that the outcome of training is more easily assessed. The benefit to learners is that they know what is expected of them.

Learner profile

Designers of learning materials need to find out as much as possible about their proposed group of learners – in other words, they need to draw up learner profiles. More specifically, they should:

▮ identify the gap between the required standards of performance or competencies and learners' current performance
▮ influence the training approach and the type of media used
▮ determine how the training materials are to be developed and delivered.

Here is a list of a few techniques for gathering information on prospective learners:

1   Write down all you know about the target audience, drawing on any previous knowledge you have of these learners (or similar groups). Check that the information is up to date!

2   Collect and analyse any written information available, eg relevant statistics or reports. This approach can also identify performance (and other) issues that may need to be discussed further with learners or their managers (or both).

3   Observe how tasks are performed; the output (where measurable); how the relevant competencies are performed; and (if applicable) how equipment is utilised. This information should then be verified.

4   Interview individually or in groups prospective learners and those who know them (eg colleagues and managers). Identify what they would like to get out of the training event, and find out what their existing knowledge and skills are.

Keep in touch with learners during the training through tutorials or coaching sessions, by telephone, at meetings, or by reading, and commenting on, their assignments. This may help you improve upon the materials for future use.

The type of information you need about learners depends on the materials to be developed. As a starting-point I often use a check-list (like that in Table 2 opposite) to identify which characteristics I should be looking for, and to stimulate ideas. (Not all may be relevant to your situation and, equally, you may wish to add some of your own.)

There are many ways you can draw up a learner profile. I tend to start by jotting down some of the key characteristics of my learners in the form of a spider diagram like the example in Figure 3 on page 10. A more detailed profile can be drawn up by putting further information against each characteristic.

Table 2

CHECK-LIST OF LEARNER CHARACTERISTICS

Demographic factors

- Number of learners and their ages
- Sex and race
- Personal disabilities/special needs
- Location(s) – where they work, where they will study
- Jobs
- Professional experience

Motivation

- Why are they learning – organisational change, change in working practices/job responsibilities?
- What are the learners'
  - needs/goals/expectations?
  - hopes and fears?
  - feelings about the proposed method/media?
- What level of motivation and confidence do they have?
- How can the proposed materials relate to their work?
- Have they experienced this type of learning before?
- Have they ever studied alone? If not, how do they feel about it?
- Do they need support?
- Will they need help in planning and managing their learning?

Subject knowledge/skills

- How do they feel about the subject being studied?
- What is their current level of skills?
- Have they any misconceptions/inappropriate habits?

- What past experience/personal interests are relevant?

Learning factors

- What are their beliefs about learning?
- What learning styles do they prefer?
- What learning skills do they have?
- What experience do they have of the proposed training method?
- Are there likely to be any problems using open learning/TBT material?
- Are there any relevant family/social circumstances?

Resources

- Where, when, and how will they be learning – at work, at home, in an open learning centre?
- What support do they require?
- What feedback from the learning event will they get?
- What access will they have to facilities/equipment/media?
- What access will they have to support – tutors, mentors, their manager?

Time-scale

- Is there a time-scale for the learning?
- How much time will they have to study at work or in their own time?

Cost

- Will they have to pay for their own training?

Figure 3

INDUCTION PROGRAMME – LEARNER PROFILE

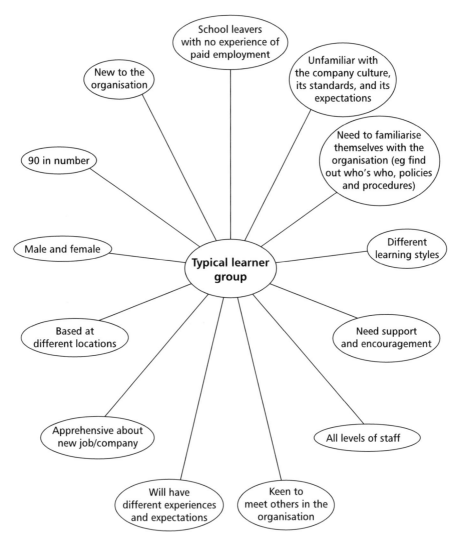

Profiles can highlight characteristics that may have a bearing on how the learning materials should be developed; for example, varying levels of knowledge, skills, and attitudes may need to be catered for – you could consider including pre-tests so that individual needs can be catered for adequately. Alternatively, if all the learners come from one organisation or occupation, you could include company-specific examples.

It is important to use the information from the profile to pinpoint the performance issues where training can make the greatest – and most cost-effective – contribution. A useful starting-point is to highlight characteristics common to all the learners. Then verify your findings by discussing them with both colleagues and learners. This can avoid mistakes later on. Table 3 shows how learner characteristics may have implications for the development of a text-based open learning programme.

Table 3

ANALYSIS OF LEARNER CHARACTERISTICS

Learner characteristics	Implications for the learning material	Other implications
Different ages/ occupations	The language used within the programme should be welcoming and interesting to all parties.	
Limited time for study	The programme should be split into manageable chunks (modules) so that learners can easily study for short periods, either at work or at home.	Learners may have difficulty completing the course owing to lack of time for study or lack of motivation. Also, staffing or workloads may require adjustment to enable learners to study at work.

The outline plan

The designer needs to consider a number of important issues at this stage – the aims and objectives, outline content, appropriate training methods, the time-scale and costs, and skills and support.

Aims and objectives

Aims and objectives are the starting-point of the design process. The clearer and more measurable they are, the easier it is for the designer to write the material and assess the effectiveness of the training.

Aims are a general statement of what the learner will be able to do as a result of the training, for example:

> To demonstrate how to plan, set up, and manage a budget. Then practise the skills involved.

Objectives are more specific statements about what the learner will be able to do as a result of the training. Because they are about changing performance they need to be written in terms of the performance standards required (see page 6). Good objectives should be *clear, specific, measurable, achievable, results-oriented,* and *time-bound*. They should state:

- ▌ what learners will be able to *do* at the end of the training
- ▌ how well they will perform
- ▌ under what conditions they will perform (the conditions may affect the actual performance).

These are the three most important ingredients of a learning objective. For further information on training objectives, see Alison Hardingham's *Designing Training* (London, IPD, 1996).

The following tips will help you to write valid objectives:

1   Decide what type of learning is involved: for example, does it involve the memory, understanding, or the performance of an activity?

2   Keep this question in mind at all stages: 'How are you going to get the learner to demonstrate what has been learnt?' Start with such a statement as:

> At the end of the training session you will be able to…

> By the end of this course you will be able to…

> When you have completed this unit, you will be able to...

You can then go into more detail.

3   For a lengthy training programme you may want to consider having an overall objective at the start, with subobjectives that together lead to achievement of the overall objective. This makes it easier to assess the outcomes.

4   Look for 'action' words to describe what you want learners to be able to do on completion of their training. A good objective might state, for example, that learners are to 'apply the terms and conditions of service in an equitable way to all employees'. 'Apply' is a good 'action' word. A weak word, by contrast, is 'appreciate', as in this example of a poor objective: learners are to 'appreciate what the terms and conditions of service are'. How can you measure such an appreciation? What does it really mean in this context? Table 4 on page 14 lists useful action words – and also words to be avoided.

Outline content

The scene has been set – the designer has a clear idea of what the learners should be able to do on completion of training, and is now in a position to draw up an outline plan of the content. To do this, the designer must first consider what the learners need to be taught in order to meet the objectives. The outline content may be subject-oriented (aimed at changing views or ideas) or learner-centred (to help learners change their performance and attidudes etc). In a lot of situations both will probably be required to differing degrees.

Ideas for content can come from brainstorming, the use of existing materials, drawing on your knowledge about the subject, research, or by discussion with colleagues. As a start, list the headings of the main topics to be covered

Table 4

WRITING OBJECTIVES

Action words			
Conceptual	*Informational*	*Skill objectives*	
∎ Analyse	∎ Classify	∎ Build	∎ Modify
∎ Apply	∎ Contrast	∎ Choose	∎ Order
∎ Compare	∎ Define	∎ Code	∎ Point
∎ Contrast	∎ Describe	∎ Connect	∎ Print
∎ Evaluate	∎ Discuss	∎ Create	∎ Repeat
∎ Interpret	∎ Explain	∎ Delete	∎ Save
∎ Investigate	∎ Identify	∎ Demonstrate	∎ Select
∎ Prioritise	∎ List	∎ Design	∎ Sort
∎ Produce	∎ Outline	∎ Duplicate	∎ State
∎ Solve		∎ Edit	
		∎ Identify	
Words to avoid			
∎ Acquire	∎ Be aware of	∎ Understand	
∎ Appreciate	∎ Familiarise		

in the training event and the sequence in which they will be dealt (ie an outline programme). Bear in mind that the content should be:

∎ relevant

∎ adequate for the learner to meet the stated objectives

∎ able to deal with potential problems that the trainer and the learner (or both) may have in coping with the material

∎ flexible, so that it can satisfy differing training needs.

Realistic timings for completion of the training should also be set.

Appropriate training methods

It is generally acknowledged that learning is a continuous process that can take many forms, not just the conventional ones (eg with a teacher in a classroom). So the designer has a number of choices when selecting training methods – role-plays, business games, text-based open learning, and TBT to name but a few. (Some of the most commonly used learning materials are discussed in Chapters 4 to 7.) The benefits of each method should be considered in the light of your situation, budget, and time-scales. Any one method need not be intrinsically better than another, but, obviously, some are more appropriate for certain learning situations. Points to consider when selecting a training method are:

▋ the type of learning involved
▋ whether it truly supports the learning objectives, ie helps learners to meet them
▋ what is easily accessible to learners – can employees at remote sites easily attend a central open learning centre to make use of TBT?
▋ whether the people who are to deliver the training have the skills to do so
▋ whether the cost is within your budget
▋ how learning can be transferred to the workplace, eg by using work-based activities, projects, and assignments.

Time-scales and costs

Realistic time-scales need to be set for the development of materials. Consider how long it will take to write, develop, and produce the product, and set a commencement and achievement date. It is all too easy to underestimate the complexity of the development and production process. Both are very labour-intensive tasks involving a lot of man-hours, so build into your project as much time as possible for each phase.

Costs can vary tremendously from a few pounds to many thousands for a TBT programme. The actual cost will depend on many variables, such as what training method you adopt, whether you develop the materials in-house or use an outside company, the type of media used, the quality you require in presentation or speed of delivery (in the case of TBT), and the resources and skills required. For example, to develop a two-hour CD-ROM program could take five or six months and cost as much as £250,000 (1996 prices), depending on the specification.

Consider whether you need to include any of the costs listed below:

■ *people*, eg specialists to design, write, edit, or test the programme; project managers and administrators
■ *resources*, eg hardware (for development and delivery); teaching materials; an authoring system (to develop TBT); software
■ *training*, to give people the knowledge and skills required to develop the materials
■ *production costs*, eg video or audio production; graphic design; materials (paper, ringbinders etc); printing
■ *copyright fees*
■ *the learning environment*, eg study area, open learning centre, resource library
■ *on-going costs*, eg for equipment (including maintenance); tutor support; updating materials.

It is worth including 10 per cent in the budget for contingencies (especially for larger projects). With the best will in the world, requirements sometimes change and it would be a shame if a worthwhile programme could not be completed simply because the budget had been carried out inadequately.

Skills and support

There may be occasions when you do not have the necessary skills to develop the materials you have selected, eg to produce a video, text-based open learning, or TBT, and therefore need to rely on help from other professionals (internal or external). Consider also whether you will need to update the material, and how much that will cost.

Learners need support. The type of support that they need could affect both how you develop the materials and their cost, and it can come in many forms:

∎ guidance on learning options, eg selection of open learning material

∎ how to use a training package most effectively

∎ drawing up a development plan in agreement (normally) between the manager or trainer and the learner

∎ providing coaching/mentor/tutor support

∎ recording learners' progress

∎ facilitating feedback, face to face or in written form.

In terms of support, where learners study – the learning environment – is another important consideration. From the employer's point of view there may be logistical constraints on providing conventional training at set locations, or allocating a dedicated room for TBT.

Once the specification has been drawn up, get the agreement and commitment of all those involved before the detailed design and development commence. This helps to avoid misunderstandings.

Selecting appropriate materials
The options

The outline plan that you should have already developed may affect your selection of materials: it is no use considering whether to customise a TBT package if your budget is very restricted, for example. There are three main options: to purchase 'generic', off-the-shelf materials; to customise something that already exists; or to develop a course for your own needs – a bespoke product.

Each option has its advantages. Off-the-shelf materials save time and money because there is no development stage. Such material can be had from sources both within and outside the organisation concerned. Internal sources may provide activities from training sessions, company documents, procedures specific to the organisation, and in-house databases. External sources include generic packages, current legislation, codes of practice, and (of course) books, journals, audiocassettes, and videos. Many of you may already have good working relationships with suppliers and producers of materials and therefore know where to go for information. For those who are looking for additional sources, you could try:

- colleagues
- contacts within other organisations
- training directories and yearbooks
- suppliers' catalogues
- publishers' catalogues
- professional journals, eg the IPD's *People Management*
- libraries
- conferences and exhibitions
- training consultancies
- professional bodies such as the IPD.

The advantage of customising existing materials is that they can be tailored to your learners' needs and be piloted (and, after feedback has been given, improved) to ensure that your objectives have been met. Materials can be customised piecemeal, again saving time and money. You can adapt material (which may involve getting copyright permission – see below) and then build training around it, eg by including customised modules, workbooks, examples, illustrations, and learning activities in your own training material.

There may be occasions, however, when a bespoke product is the best way to meet your needs – for instance, if information has to be highly specific to the organisation's procedures, equipment, services, and products.

Once you have chosen the kind of material that you want, you have to decide whether a particular example of it measures up to your purposes. To make this decision you have to set quality criteria.

Quality criteria

Clearly you have to satisfy yourself that a given training package or resource is appropriate for your purposes, ie establish your quality criteria. A useful way to do this is simply to list what you feel are a given package's good and bad features. To get you started, Table 5 on page 20 provides a check-list of some quality criteria. Bear in mind that, along with these criteria, you should also consider such matters as your own aims and objectives, the proposed learning environments, and your budget.

Copyright

When developing any type of learning materials you should always get copyright permission if you intend to use other people's work. This should be done even if you intend to use only a small part of a given work – say, one page of a book or just one photograph (or even a detail from a phtograph). This can be expensive, but it is still probably cheaper than producing your own material from scratch.

In the UK the appropriate legislation covering this subject is the Copyright and Data Protection Act 1988. Copyright covers not just books, but also sound recordings, videos, films, music, photographs, and computer programs, among other works, and is invoked to stop people copying others' works without permission. Protection of authors lasts the life of the author and 50 years thereafter, for example. In the case of multimedia, copyright is complex: you may be looking at copyright for soundtracks, music, photographs, video footage, and graphics. In-house developers of learning materials should therefore be fully aware

Table 5

CHECK-LIST OF QUALITY CRITERIA

Aims and objectives

- Clear and measurable (overall and for each module/session)
- Meets the objectives set out in the specification

Content

- Clear instructions on how to use the materials
- Relevant and up to date
- Tells you where to get information
- The subject matter specified in the initial objectives is covered in detail
- Good supporting information, eg for the trainer/facilitator/mentor/learner

Structure and organisation

- Clearly defined
- Logical sequences between modules
- Can be updated
- Can be customised

Learner control

- Flexible access
- Training can be tailored to meet a learner's specific needs

Exercises and activities

- Clear instructions on how to complete activities, how feedback will be given, and the time required to complete it
- Allows for a mixture of views and answers
- Starts with simple questions, then builds towards more complex activities

- Allows for reviewing/positive feedback by trainer/facilitator, or builds this into the material itself
- Interactive
- User-friendly
- Enjoyable

Appearance

- Attractive
- Self-explanatory
- Consistent presentation
- Good use of colour, highlighting, graphics, illustrations
- Appropriate typographic style and size
- Printed material is well spaced out
- Text is split into manageable chunks (modules)
- Clear headings and subheadings

Language

- Aimed at the right level
- Easy to understand
- Friendly and informal tone
- Technical terms and jargon clearly explained

Support

- Adequate support provided, eg in the form of a trainer/facilitator/ coach/mentor; material built into the programme (eg text-based open learning or TBT); on-line help facilities (TBT) of what is in the public domain and what remains under copyright. Clearly, the more you can produce in-house, the less you need to worry about infringing the law.

Today copyright is an important economic issue. TBT producers, video makers, publishers, and computer software manufacturers – to name a few – depend on it to remain commercially viable. They need to protect themselves against unauthorised copying of their work. Bear in mind that in some areas there are further, similar rights to consider, such as the rights of broadcasters to protect their work against those who receive cable transmissions illegally, and the field of intellectual property rights.

Producers of training materials are as keen as anyone to protect their copyright. Whereas producers of printed material can do little more than put a copyright notice (©) on pages, TBT packages sometimes make use of security devices such as restrictions on certain parts of a program (if the package is out on evaluation), 'time elapses' (allowing access for a limited period, eg 14 days), or a 'dongle' (a removable encoded hardware device that restricts the use of software-based packages). Generic learning materials are normally copyright-protected unless there is a specific statement that all, or parts of them, may be photocopied. Course notes and handouts and resource packs may usually be photocopied with impunity, as may workbooks accompanying TBT packages, but always check first!

In brief

- Before detailed work can be commenced, the designer needs to put together a design specification taking account of learning needs, competencies, learner profiles, objectives, content, time-scales, costs, and resources.
- The designer has three main options when selecting materials: to purchase generic, off-the-shelf materials, to customise existing materials, or to develop a bespoke product.

∎ Learning materials should be selected according to your objectives, the target audience, quality criteria, learning environment, and budget.

∎ Always check whether materials are copyright-protected before you use them in any way.

2 Developing Your Materials

Introduction

The design stage is crucial. It is here that you decide on the content of your learning materials – and without good content you will not meet your objectives. In this chapter I shall discuss project-planning, setting quality standards, design considerations, guidelines on writing materials, and testing and monitoring materials.

The project plan

The project plan defines the tasks involved and the order in which they are to be completed. With a large project, you may want to consider appointing a manager to oversee the process, ie resource the project, set up a team, draw up a project plan, and ensure that time-scales are met and that the project is kept within budget.

Project-planning is a subject in its own right, so I intend merely to touch on the subject here, to get you started. All plans consist of core factors such as budgets, communications, resources (people and equipment), and quality controls as well as some features unique to the particular project, such as the tasks involved, the structure, and the strategy. A typical project-planning process is shown in Figure 4 on page 24.

Figure 4

PLANNING STAGES

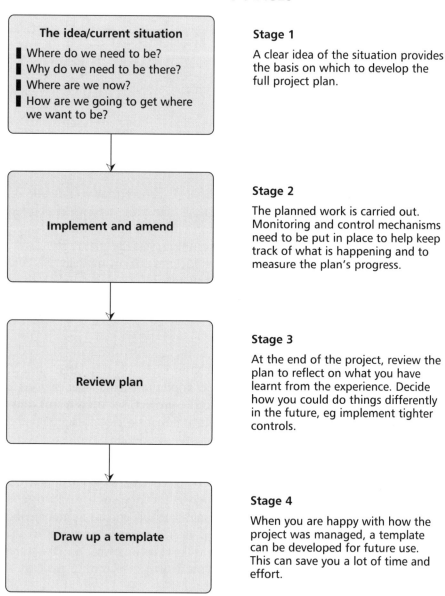

The idea/current situation

▮ Where do we need to be?
▮ Why do we need to be there?
▮ Where are we now?
▮ How are we going to get where we want to be?

Stage 1

A clear idea of the situation provides the basis on which to develop the full project plan.

Implement and amend

Stage 2

The planned work is carried out. Monitoring and control mechanisms need to be put in place to help keep track of what is happening and to measure the plan's progress.

Review plan

Stage 3

At the end of the project, review the plan to reflect on what you have learnt from the experience. Decide how you could do things differently in the future, eg implement tighter controls.

Draw up a template

Stage 4

When you are happy with how the project was managed, a template can be developed for future use. This can save you a lot of time and effort.

When identifying the current situation, I find the SWOT (Strengths, Weaknesses, Opportunities, and Threats) analysis technique useful. This technique is used widely in various training situations. (The design specification discussed in Chapter 1 will also help.)

If you are planning a project at the moment, try using the SWOT analysis to consider whether any internal or external factors may affect the development of the materials in the short or long term. This will help your development strategy. An example of a SWOT analysis is set out in Figure 5.

Figure 5

SWOT ANALYSIS

Strengths	Opportunities
▌ The writing skills required to develop the text-based open learning package are available in-house.	▌ A colleague in another division is planning to develop similar materials in the next month or two, so there may be an opportunity to share ideas and materials.
Weaknesses	**Threats**
▌ There are few existing materials available that can be used.	▌ New legislation to be implemented over the next two to three months is likely to affect the content.

The level of detail in your project plan depends on the complexity of the materials being developed, eg:

▌ the tasks that need to be done to complete the product

▌ how long each task will take

▌ the resources required, eg materials, equipment, and people

■ the cost of carrying out the different tasks
■ the number of people who need to be kept informed, and how and when
■ the target dates for completion
■ the standards of quality required.

From the answers to such questions a *project plan* can be drawn up of how you intend to reach your desired outcome – the completed materials. This can provide a framework within which the project manager co-ordinates the different tasks involved, monitors progress, tests and modifies the materials, and produces them. An example project plan can be seen in Figure 6.

Figure 6

EXAMPLE 'PROJECT PLAN'

Task no.	Task description	Who is responsible?	Whose agreement is needed?	Target date
10.	To set objectives for each module.	Trainer.	Managers involved.	31 July.

Communications play an important part in project management. Wherever you are in a project, you need to keep yourself informed about what is going on within the organisation, eg in terms of changes. Any possible consequences should be kept in mind and monitored, and the project plan updated as necessary.

Setting quality standards

To ensure the effectiveness of your materials and the service of those supplying them (writers, developers, producers, and printers), quality standards should be established. Not only do they provide a useful benchmark against which you can monitor the development of the materials, they can also be used to evaluate the materials at the sign-off stage. Quality standards regarding a course might state, for example, that it be competency-based with optional pre- or post-testing and administration, and meet the NVQ (national vocational qualification) standards laid down by the appropriate lead body.

The aim of setting standards is to meet your (or the sponsor's) requirements. As far as possible, judgements should be quantifiable, but you may find that some are not easy to quantify, eg judgements about layout, appearance, and durability. Common control measures are: quality (eg does the product meet the requirements?), time, cost, and quantity. Usually a combination of such measures is required in any control system (eg measuring quality against cost).

Because people's perceptions differ, it is worth gaining agreement on the quality standards between all the parties involved. Some areas for which you may find it useful to set quality standards are set out in Table 6 on page 28, taking a technology-based training package as an example.

Design principles

The effectiveness of learning materials – whether they meet the objectives – depends on the designer. He or she has to ensure that learners acquire the skills, knowledge, or behaviour that will improve performance. Good design principles must therefore be followed, based on a learning model. A simple learning model might be to provide the learner with:

▌ information
▌ opportunities to try out what has been learnt
▌ a summary of what has been learnt.

Table 6

AREAS FOR SETTING QUALITY STANDARDS

■ **Content**. Is the material aimed at the right level; split into manageable chunks; in a logical sequence? Is it accurate, current, and clearly presented? Does it relate to the real world?

■ **Flexibility**, eg in terms of providing as much or as little study material as the learner needs or time allows. Is there flexible access to the different parts of the course, ie have learners the ability to move forwards, backwards, pause, exit the course, change modules/topics?

■ **Structure/organisation**. Is a clearly defined course structure for each module provided? Is the material consistent and in a logical sequence? Are there links between modules? Does the structure support learners and provide guided-learning paths based on learners' responses? Can the program be easily updated?

■ **Learner control**. What control do learners have over *what* and *how* they learn?

■ **Interface design and human factors**. Is it user-friendly, aesthetically pleasing, and suited to learners' culture and prior knowledge? Consider also (where appropriate) the quality of the acting and the suitability of the presenters.

■ **Screen format**. Is it appealing? Does it keep learners' attention? Does it reinforce learners' positive attitudes to the medium? Is effective use made of the screen, eg good use of colour, consistent and effective use of typeface and graphics, images, motion video, and audio?

■ **Linking**. (Cf. Flexibility.) Are the links between the program and the user set up in the right way? Do they provide learners with optional learning routes/guided-learning paths and freedom of movement? Are the links consistent? Are the ways in which the links are explained consistent, eg by menus, control/ navigational buttons, diagrams, route maps, sound, overviews, instructions on how to use the program signposting?

■ **System performance**. Is the response time fast enough? Are learners' responses stored after the system is turned off? Can the system recover from a power cut in the middle of use?

■ **Support material**. Is it integrated with other media used?

■ **Production quality**. What quality is acceptable to you for the graphic or photographic images, video, audio, or printed material?

Designers should also bear in mind:

▌ potential barriers to learning, because these may affect how the materials are developed. For example, I have heard learners comment that the language used was patronising; that they found it difficult to find their way around the course material, because it seemed to have no logical sequence and because there was no index; or that the text was a bit cluttered and, at times, difficult to read.

▌ that the three basic ingredients in any learning materials are design, content, and how the materials are worded.

▌ that learning materials need to be

clear and readable Information should be easy to read and digest, with key points highlighted and summarised.

relevant Information should be what learners need to meet their objectives.

accurate Information should be up to date, factual, in a logical sequence, and complete. If you update materials, ensure that changes are made consistently throughout.

interesting Materials should be visually attractive, making good use of design, colour, and illustrations (see Chapter 3). This will help learners to retain what they have studied.

practical Learners should be able to see clear benefits from using the materials and therefore feel more committed to them.

Session plan

The next stage is to flesh out the content of the materials, with the various parts brought together to form the complete training event. The designer should arrange these parts in a logical sequence and draw up a *session plan*. This involves:

■ setting out what people need to know

■ setting objectives for each module, topic, or activity

■ estimating the duration of each item

■ outlining the content

■ identifying appropriate training methods to meet objectives

■ deciding how the parts will be delivered.

Figure 7 shows a typical form used for session planning.

Figure 7

SESSION PLAN

Module and objectives	Estimated timing	Outline content	Method	Media/ visual aids	Delivery

If you are developing materials that include information technology (eg TBT or a computer game or simulation), a functional specification is included at this stage.

Once the session plan has been completed you should seek agreement on it from your client.

Storyboarding

Visualising how your materials will look can be hard. To help visualise and arrange content (text and illustrations), sequence events, and ensure that the information flows appropriately, I find the *storyboard* technique useful. It helps to map out the content and establish links between the information. Whether you use this technique or others (eg flipcharts or a card index) to plan the content, you should include:

▮ titles that convey what the topic is

▮ the key (content) points that the learners must remember

▮ ways in which the main points can be expressed graphically, eg with charts, bullet points, or colour.

Figure 8 gives an example of how a storyboard can look.

Figure 8

STORYBOARD (EXTRACT)

Training session/event:	
Designer:	Page of
Media:	

Content	Design layout

Title: TBT applications and uses
 	
Key points: Procedures
 	
          'Soft skills'
 	
          Theory
	Applications and uses
	
	Uses | Examples
	
	General uses will be matched against specific examples

Content

Before you develop the content, careful research needs to be carried out, bearing in mind the relevant quality standards (which you set at the start of the design stage), eg that the content should be accurate, relevant, readable, complete, and unlikely to change.

For example, let us say that a designer is developing a training programme on a new computer-based training record system which is being developed in-house. He or she collects information from the programmers and develops the materials. All the while, however, the computer department is still testing and modifying the system. At the last minute they find that some of the details of the system are inaccurate, so the designer's training materials have to be quickly amended and produced anew. A costly mistake! Adhering to the quality standards set for the content would have avoided this.

When developing content, designers should check that it is:

■ *relevant*. Will it bring value to learners in their jobs? Are learners being offered something that they really need to know? For example, someone who has to understand how to use a photocopier needs to learn about the controls, what functions are available, and how to deal with minor faults (like paper jamming) – he or she does not need to know about all the different components or how to deal with complex faults.

■ *accurate and complete*. Is the content up to date, correct, and complete? It needs to cover all the information that the learner needs to meet the objectives.

■ *stable*. Ensure that the subject matter is unlikely to change significantly (eg because of new legislation or procedures).

Writing the materials

With all this in mind, the designer is now in a position to write the materials. He or she needs to consider the following questions:

■ Which is the best way of putting the message across – text, illustrations, examples, activities and feedback, quizzes, assessment?

▌ How am I going to say it – what tone should be used?

▌ Can I express the information better with graphics than with written text – by making use of diagrams, photographs, or charts (see Chapter3)?

▌ In what format should I present the materials?

Writing effectively

To be effective, materials need be readable and interactive. They need to enhance learning – they need to motivate and encourage the learner. Materials that are unclear because they have not been thought out or because they use a lot of unexplained jargon do not make for easy reading. A few ways in which you can make your materials more readable are to:

▌ use a friendly and informal tone

▌ explain things clearly

▌ avoid overloading the learner with information

▌ use relevant anecdotes

▌ keep sentences, and paragraphs, short

▌ choose simple and familiar words

▌ avoid long phrases – say 'although' rather than 'in spite of the fact that'

▌ explain jargon and technical terms clearly.

Writing interactively

Writing interactively is important if you are asking people to complete an activity or exercise, especially in a text-based open learning programme, where learners may have little human contact. You need to establish two-way communication between the writer and reader. So try to involve and encourage participants by making use of activities and exercises and providing positive and useful feedback on them. It helps, also, if you use an informal tone. Address them in writing as you would speak to them – in a personal and direct way. This will establish a beneficial rapport between you.

Involve learners by addressing them directly – ask them for their opinions, or to think about their own situations, eg ask 'What do you think about...', 'Have you thought about...'. Naturally, your activities and exercises should be carefully worded so as to ensure that learners meet the objectives.

Checking whether your materials are readable and interactive normally happens when you are editing them or trying out ideas on colleagues and prospective learners. This is a continual process of refinement. Some questions you should ask yourself are:

I Is the material clear and easy to read?

I Are the instructions and activities clear and measurable?

I Is the content aimed at the right level and is appropriate language used?

I Is the tone friendly and unpatronising?

I Are technical terms and jargon clearly explained?

I Is the feedback from activities and questions helpful to the learner?

Writing learning activities

People tend to learn more if they are active rather than passive. Activities can be used as part of group and individual learning sessions, text-based open learning, TBT – in fact, in all manner of learning methods. A typical approach to developing activities is shown in Figure 9 opposite.

Activities can benefit learners by providing:

I clear instructions (briefs for participants and observers, facilitator guides)

I variety

I opportunities to practise

I positive and useful feedback (letting learners know what they are doing right, and what could be improved upon).

Figure 9

HOW TO DEVELOP LEARNING ACTIVITIES

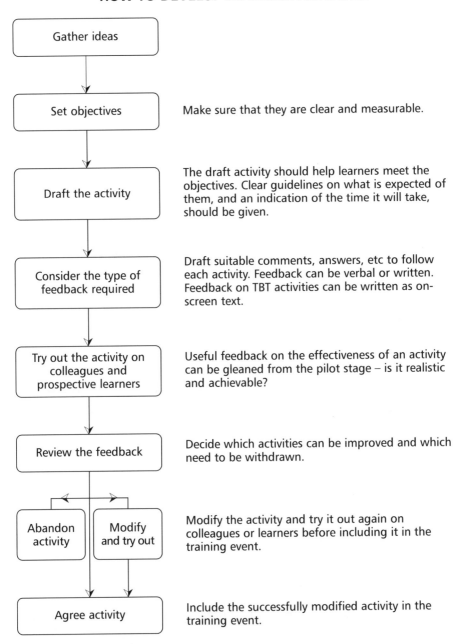

Gather ideas

Set objectives — Make sure that they are clear and measurable.

Draft the activity — The draft activity should help learners meet the objectives. Clear guidelines on what is expected of them, and an indication of the time it will take, should be given.

Consider the type of feedback required — Draft suitable comments, answers, etc to follow each activity. Feedback can be verbal or written. Feedback on TBT activities can be written as on-screen text.

Try out the activity on colleagues and prospective learners — Useful feedback on the effectiveness of an activity can be gleaned from the pilot stage – is it realistic and achievable?

Review the feedback — Decide which activities can be improved and which need to be withdrawn.

Abandon activity | Modify and try out — Modify the activity and try it out again on colleagues or learners before including it in the training event.

Agree activity — Include the successfully modified activity in the training event.

Before we go on, this last point (about feedback) should perhaps be underlined: feedback is important and should be positive and satisfying, help to identify an individual's strengths and weaknesses, and highlight the areas that learners need to concentrate on. It should:

▮ acknowledge the effort that learners have put in
▮ give reassurance and encouragement
▮ indicate strengths and weaknesses
▮ give clear advice on how weaknesses can be remedied
▮ give opportunities to raise problems and queries.

Titles and introductions

First impressions are important. The first contact your learners will have with your materials is the title and introduction. These should catch people's attention and give them an idea of what is to come. Titles should be brief, arouse interest, tell learners what the materials are about, and be meaningful in their own right. Introductions should set both the scene and the mood in which learners will proceed. They should include:

▮ an outline of the topic and its purpose
▮ an explanation of what participants will be doing and how
▮ guidelines on the use and structure of the package, eg examples of learning pathways.

Where support materials are included in the package (as with a text-based open learning package), the main introduction may be in the form of a learner guide which gives an overview of the complete course. If this is the case, you might consider also having an introduction to each module workbook, with a brief description on the topic to set the scene.

With TBT, the introduction is likely to be found either in accompanying support literature or as an integral part of the program itself. Support literature should include clear guidelines on the system requirements for the software, how much space you will need on the hard disk, and installation instructions. Other guidelines may also be necessary on how to use the mouse; the course structure and content; how learners can find their way around the program (eg navigational aids); and help facilities.

Testing and monitoring

During the development stage you should continually be testing and monitoring your materials by trying out ideas and activities on colleagues or prospective learners, remembering of course to measure the results against the quality standards. When you have finally developed the content, ask colleagues to review it and give you feedback. Can they see any areas that may cause trainees problems? Can they think of any useful anecdotes to put in? Are they aware of any short- or long-term initiatives that may affect the materials? Existing materials should also be reviewed and validated: there may be ways in which you can be more creative and build in improvements.

Piloting your materials

It is advisable to carry out a controlled pilot involving learners similar to the target audience. To evaluate the effectiveness of the materials, get the 'guinea pig' learners to work through the course and make notes of any problems. You may find it useful to review the learners' comments with them and ask for suggestions. Additional feedback can often be obtained this way. (If piloting an open learning programme, you may need to provide a tutor and other forms of support in addition to the text-based self-study materials.)

When running a pilot, you should clearly brief the learners involved, eg tell them why they are taking part; give them information on the course programme or activity; tell them how to use the equipment (if needed); how to get the most out of the training event; and how the feedback on the course will be used.

Evaluation after the event

Having successfully piloted and carried out your training programme, you now want to know whether it did the job: you need to evaluate it, in other words. So what is evaluation? Effective training is about making a difference and evaluation is about assessing that difference. The difference may show itself in improved performance on the job; demonstration of competence in a job; improved knowledge or skills; or a change in attitude and behaviour.

Evaluation is a continual process of checking the effectiveness of the materials against the quality standards, and of modifying them as a result of feedback. Those elements that worked well can be used again; those that did not can be removed. Other ideas for improvement may also come out of the evaluation. This process is largely driven by the trainer, who uses it to gauge performance, the value of the training to the organisation, and cost-effectiveness. When designing evaluation methods, you may want to consider such questions as:

▮ What do I want to evaluate?

▮ Why do I want to evaluate it?

▮ When shall I evaluate?

▮ Who needs to know the findings? Take into account the concerns of all interested parties when designing your evaluation methods.

▮ How shall I collect the information?

▮ Where will the information be collected?

▮ How will the findings be presented?

▮ How will the findings be used?

Numerous evaluation methods exist:

▮ support systems as part of the course. In the case of an open-learning pilot, additional feedback can be gained from learners during one-to-one tutorials and workshops.

▮ evaluation questionnaires (paper-based or computerised).

These can be issued to learners on completion of the training event – and in a way that demonstrates they are important and not just an afterthought. Consider briefing learners on why feedback is required, eg to assess whether the learning materials are effective or, if they are lacking, to highlight ways in which they can be improved.

∎ student-tracking systems (TBT). Some computer-based training (CBT) and CD-ROM packages have a student-tracking system that records and displays results. The amount of information held on these systems varies, but they can be useful as part of the evaluation process. They can record:

☐ course usage and time spent on different sections. By recording the time a learner takes to complete different parts of the course, the designer can highlight areas of difficulty.

☐ a learner's route through the program and their test results. These could show whether the course structure and materials are effective.

☐ learners' responses to questions. This can show the strengths and weaknesses of individual learners, and how (or whether) their performance has improved as a result of completing the course.

An example access screen from a student tracking system from a Xebec package is set out in Figure 10 on page 40.

∎ work-based activities and projects. On completion of training, you may consider asking learners to complete work-based activities or a project in order to help them apply to their jobs what they have learnt, and in order to demonstrate that the desired competencies have been reached.

∎ reviews with learners. Reviews normally take place some time after the training to assess how performance has changed. The main disadvantage of this approach is however that many features of the course may not

Figure 10

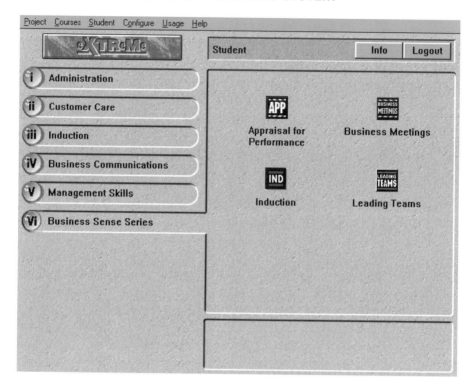

ACCESS (MENU SELECTION) SCREEN FROM A STUDENT-TRACKING SYSTEM

be discussed or may simply be forgotten owing to the passage of time or pressures of work.

Feedback from the pilot helps to gauge the effectiveness of the materials as a whole. Further modifications can be made, if necessary, to ensure that objectives are more closely met in the future. If you would like to find out more about how to validate and evaluate training, a useful reference book is *Evaluating Training* by Peter Bramley (London, IPD, 1996).

Once you are happy with the materials, they can be signed off and produced.

In brief

▌ Drawing up a project plan involves: defining tasks, prioritising them, setting target dates, and identifying necessary resources.

▌ Quality standards provide a benchmark against which you can monitor the effectiveness of the materials being developed.

▌ Potential barriers to learning include poor presentation and irrelevant content. These should be addressed when developing your materials.

▌ Learning materials should be clear, readable, relevant, accurate, interesting, and practical.

▌ Materials can be made readable by using a friendly and informal tone; by clearly explaining things; by keeping sentences short; and by using appropriate language.

▌ Writing can be made interactive by making use of a range of activities and providing feedback; by establishing a relationship with the learner; by talking to the learner directly in order to involve him or her; and by developing carefully worded activities.

▌ Testing and monitoring is a continuous process during which the materials are measured against the quality standards.

▌ There are a variety of techniques that can be used to evaluate training, eg questionnaires, reviews, work-based activities, and projects.

3

Guidelines on Graphic Design and Printing

Materials need to be attractively presented in order to help learners retain what they have studied. In this chapter, therefore, I aim to provide you with some ideas on how to come up with attractive and eye-catching design solutions.

Deciding on your format

The overall appearance of your materials should never distract learners from the lesson in hand. The format you choose should:

- be clean and clear
- have a pleasing layout
- use appropriate colours and illustrations
- promote a desire to learn
- create an image of professionalism.

When you are deciding on the appropriate format, imagine that you are assembling a picture that consists of different parts all needing to fit together harmoniously. What this means is that you need to understand the building blocks of graphic design and use them appropriately for the project you are working on. The type of format you choose depends on the materials you are developing. In the case of printed learning materials (the most commonly used type) there an several key points to consider:

Purpose	Be clear about what you want to achieve. Take into account the media being used and the messages you want to convey. This is essential if you are to know how to lay your materials out, what to include, and where to position photographs and other illustrations.
Experimentation	Ideas for layout come from experimenting and brainstorming. Try out different ideas by sketching them on a piece of paper to see what they look like. You do not have to go into any detail at this stage – just doodle, eg depict text by lines, and illustrations and photographs by a box with a very rough sketch inside.
Relevance	All the elements in your design should be relevant to your objectives and audience. They should help learners understand and retain the messages conveyed.
Proportion	The size of the elements that make up your material should be determined by their importance (the size of typeface and headlines, illustrations, etc).
Direction	Effective design should direct learners through the materials, making it easy for them to move around and find the information they require.
Consistency	Consistency means producing an integrated style in terms of size of typeface, spacing, use of white space, headlines and subheadings,

style of paragraph, borders, etc. As far as possible be consistent in your approach to:

- typeface, typestyle, and size
- the number of colours used, eg for headings, subtitles, text, and background colour
- headings and subheadings
- how text is formatted, eg in terms of margins and line-spacing
- bullet points
- borders, boxes, and tints.

Contrast

Building visual contrast into your materials makes the information more interesting and eye-catching. You may want to consider making titles larger than the text, or presenting figures and percentages as a graph or chart.

Simplicity

Decide which design most effortlessly enhances the message you want to convey and meets the objectives.

Keeping these considerations in mind, let us now look at some of the building blocks of graphic design.

Building blocks of graphic design

Materials can be made to look more attractive and interesting by using a variety of techniques. As you read through this section, think about some materials you are currently developing, or need to update, and consider how you might improve the design.

Layout

There are two possible layouts:

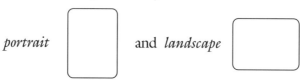

portrait   and *landscape*

Text-based materials are usually presented in the portrait layout. If you use this for slides and overhead transparencies (OHTs), you may find yourself having to use a smaller typeface, which may in turn leave the message hard to read at a distance. With a landscape layout, you are more restricted in the amount of information you can put on the slide, but a larger typesize can be used, making the text clearer and more readable.

Typography

Typography refers to the appearance of letters, numbers, and other characters. A particular set of such letters is called a typeface; your choice of typeface, its size, and how it is set out influence the appearance of individual pages and indeed of the material as a whole. The typeface can communicate an attitude that may either help or hinder learners' ability to understand your message and retain it. These are some of the factors that should influence your choice of typeface:

- *the media* – printed material, visual aids, TBT, etc. For example, sans serif typefaces (see below) are suitable for OHTs because they tend to be simple (ie not decorative) and so enhance legibility.
- *the tone* – do you want your material to come across as, for example, friendly, classy, decorative, or authoritative?

Serif and sans serif typefaces

Typefaces fall into two broad classes – *serif*, commonly used for text, and *sans serif*, used for display material such as headlines, subheadings, and captions. Looking at the examples of serif typefaces below in Figure 11, you will notice that they all have rounded or square strokes (serifs) at the ends of each letter. These tend to set the tone, add character to the letters, and guide the reader from letter to letter, making the text flow better. Sans serif typefaces have no such strokes and are often used for headlines, OHTs, and slides. They add impact to the message, if used in moderation.

Figure 11

EXAMPLES OF TYPEFACES

Serif typefaces	Sans serif typefaces
Times	Gill Sans
Garamond	Futura
Baskerville	Helvetica
Palatino	Univers
Bembo	Goudy Sans

Script and decorative typefaces

These are best used when an ornamental, rather than an informative, design is required. Script typefaces, as their name suggests, mimic handwriting; they can create an impression of elegance (eg *Zapf Chancery*) or informality (eg *Brush*), adding variety to texts and a pleasing contrast to more conventional typefaces. Decorative typefaces are highly individualistic styles that should perhaps be used sparingly, although they too can create a dramatic effect, if that is what you want.

Type style

By type style I mean the different versions you can find of the same typeface. Typefaces are usually available in roman and italic versions, which use letters of the standard thickness for the particular typeface. Roman letters are vertical, like the ones you are reading now, *whereas italic letters slant*, and can be used to highlight words. The thickness of the letters can be increased, however, to produce either **bold roman** or ***bold italic***, providing more punch to the affected words. Bold obviously makes text stand out, but use it sparingly: too much can make a page look heavy and dark. A good general tip is to use italic within your main text and use bold for headings.

Typesize

Typesize is measured in units called points – 72 pts equals roughly 1 inch. Most word-processing packages can go up to this size, but most printed material (books, handouts etc) appear in 10 or 11 point type. The typesize used in your materials should be determined by:

■ the media – a larger typesize will be needed for OHTs and slides (because they will be viewed from a distance) than for handout material

■ the importance of your message

■ the amount of white space available

■ the width and number of columns used in printed material.

Avoid obvious errors such as putting a few words in small point size in the middle of a lot of white space, so that it looks lost; equally, do not cram words into a small space, reducing legibility and irritating your readers. Try to get a balance.

Alignment

Text can be justified right or left or have a ragged margin, and in either case may be centred. A ragged edge gives a feeling of 'openness' (the lines are of unequal length), whereas justified text (like that on this page) produces lines of equal length. I find when producing handouts or other printed materials that text works best if it is justified.

Paragraphs, spacing, and indents

Spacing between words, lines, and paragraphs needs to be consistent throughout your materials. Used judiciously, it creates a feeling of openness and breaks up the density of large blocks of text, improving readability. Unbroken blocks of text can be hard on the eye and difficult to read. When writing materials, I find that lines no longer than 60 to 70 characters, wide margins, and the use of indents make reading easier. Long lines of text can be tiring on the eye.

Another helpful way to break up your text and keep readers' attention is to use bullet points (such as those used in this book). These highlight a number of related points or a sequence of events, and many software programs offer them in a variety of styles.

White space

As a designer of materials your aim is to make them interesting. White space can help you do so because it adds contrast and a resting-place for readers' eyes. This does not mean leaving large areas of a page blank; it means instead creating space in different ways, eg

- around a heading
- by using page margins, space between columns, or ragged line-endings, which can relieve the monotony of large areas of justified text
- indented paragraphs.

Borders, boxes, and tints

The use of borders and box frames draws attention to an area of work and highlights specific parts of the material, eg a photograph or illustration. For example, 'drop shadow' boxes can attractively frame a visual.

Example of a

drop-shadow box

If including tips, quotations, or case-studies in your material, why not consider using tints to highlight them? It would help readers quickly to recognise them as they work through the material.

Headers and footers

A header (also called a running head or running headline) is the title of a book (or manual, workbook, etc) repeated at the top of every left-hand page of text, with the chapter or section heading on the right-hand page. If this feature appears at the foot of a page it is called, logically, a footer. Headers and footers can be very helpful to let readers find out quickly which module or chapter is being covered.

Company logos

You can establish an identity for your materials by including your company logo on the front cover.

Icons

Icons are often used to help readers find their way around by referring to specific sections of the materials, eg activities, summaries, or check-lists. In text-based open learning and TBT, they are used as navigational aids. A few examples are:

 Video

 Audio

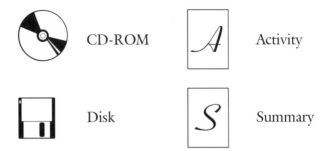

CD-ROM   Activity

Disk   Summary

Graphics

Line drawings, photographs, diagrammatic illustrations, cartoons, and charts are all graphic material that may be used for many different purposes in all types of media. With multimedia, animation and video sequences can enhance the effectiveness of your message and make the screen visually more attractive. Illustrations can be created by hand (eg a drawing) or be computer-generated. In the latter case ready-made 'clip art' (on a floppy disk or a CD-ROM) not only saves time and effort but also enlivens your presentation. Clip art often covers such different themes as occupations, the office, animals, and holidays. If you intend to use graphics, bear in mind these tips:

▮ Use them only when necessary, ie to help readers *understand* something.

▮ Photographs are useful for showing an event or to portray a situation not normally accessible, eg parts of equipment, or health and safety hazards.

▮ Diagrammatic illustrations are a good way of depicting a complex object such as an organisational structure or a flowchart of a course structure.

▮ Leave reasonable space around your graphics so the eye moves to them naturally.

▮ Be consistent in how you present graphics.

▮ Avoid complex charts and diagrams – they can be confusing and distracting.

▮ Enhance the visual impact of your graphs by using

larger typefaces to improve legibility.

■ Grid lines can help viewers focus on the data.

Charts and graphs

Charts and graphs are used to interpret and display information, eg trends, or comparisons of data. Pie charts display percentages of a whole, for example (see figure 12).

Figure 12

BREAKDOWN OF TRAINING DELIVERY

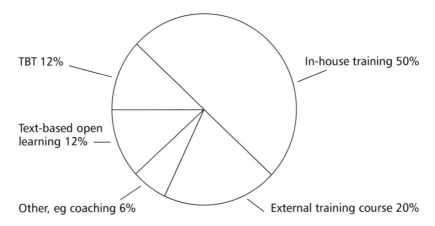

TBT 12%

In-house training 50%

Text-based open learning 12%

Other, eg coaching 6%

External training course 20%

Bar graphs can attractively present results of sales or display statistics; or may be used to compare information such as age distribution in different departments, or sales results over the last five years (see Figure 13 on page 52). Line graphs illustrate trends such as labour turnover within an organisation (see Figure 14 on page 52).

Colours

Colour can lend a strong impact to your materials. They can capture learners' attention, create a mood, and simply make things look more attractive. But how do you go about choosing a colour? Bear in mind that some colours

Figure 13

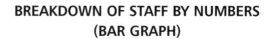

**BREAKDOWN OF STAFF BY NUMBERS
(BAR GRAPH)**

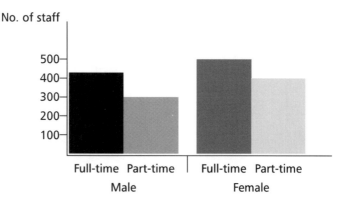

Figure 14

RATE OF LABOUR TURNOVER (LINE GRAPH)

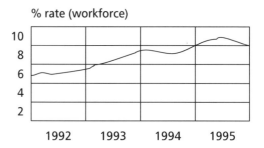

arouse certain connotations. Red, for instance, shouts for attention and can be overpowering if used too liberally; in financial terms it can signify a problem, such as debt. Green tends to be relaxing and reassuring, conjuring ideas of the environment and health. Grey and black may appear sombre, even depressing, but can also lend a quiet dignity to the page, if that is the effect you want to achieve. The other, highly important, factor to bear in mind is of course your budget. The cost is of course greater to print in two or more colours rather than one.

If you are using an actual colour press (rather than, say, a colour printer attached to your personal computer) you need to know how to specify colours in the appropriate way. It is no use asking a printer to provide you with a 'light green' book cover, for example: *how* light, what *shade* of green are you after?

Your choice is between 'special' (or 'spot') colours that have to be mixed and 'process' colours made by printing different combinations of yellow, magenta, cyan, and black (the so-called process colours, used in most colour printing). If you want to match a specific colour it is probably easiest if you match it against a sample collection such as the Pantone Matching System (PMS, a colour-matching standard used by designers and print-buyers). Each colour has a number that identifies it and so gives the printer an exact idea of the desired result. (Pantone 185, for example, refers to a particular shade of red.)

It is cheaper, and usually sufficient for most purposes, to have just black and one special or spot colour; this is called two-colour printing. The special colour can be used for tints or charts; to underline text; to highlight specific information; or to make headings stand out. Your materials can be made much more inviting by such use of a second colour.

Tinting colours

To create the illusion of several shades of a colour within a document you can *tint* a special colour. This means using a percentage (a lower tonal value) of the particular colour. The obvious example is to take black and reduce its percentage from 100 to, say, 20, so that the illusion of grey is produced (see Figure 15 on page 54). Similarly you can produce light and dark greens, reds, blues, etc. This effect is easy enough to achieve if you are producing materials on a colour printer attached to your personal computer, but once again you have to be more careful when using a colour press. It is probably best to talk to your proposed printer before embarking on a design that

Figure 15

SHADES OF BLACK ('TINTING')

10%		60%	
20%		80%	
40%		100%	

might turn out to be more expensive than you imagined. (You will also need to talk to the printer about the kind of paper to be used, because this might also have a bearing on the use of tinted colours.)

Colour in OHTs and slides

When using colour in OHTs you should keep the background light and the text dark, and steer away from colours that do not project well. Yellow, for example, can look pale when projected onto a screen. Slides, on the other hand, should have a dark background with light text, because this stands out better in a darkened room. The more contrast you can create between the background and the text, the better.

When selecting colours (other than black and white) on a computer you would be well advised to print them out from a colour printer before selecting them. Colours on the screen can look different when printed.

Working with printers

Printing is the last step in the development process. It is worth working closely with printers: they can give useful advice on design, materials, and other technical matters. Listening to their advice helps to ensure that the effect you want is achieved.

A normal starting-point when talking to printers is to draw up a specification in writing of your requirements. To provide you with an accurate estimate, your printer needs the exact details of the job. You should consider:

■ how the text will be provided – on disk or as camera-ready copy (either high-resolution bromide or laser printout); whenever I provide copy on disk I always check with the printer beforehand that he has the relevant software to handle it

■ who will be providing any camera-ready artwork – you or the printer

■ the type of proofs and how many

■ the deadline for approving proofs – and whether they are to be backed-up or single-sided

■ the number of copies, ie the print run – and remember that it will be cheaper to print a few more copies than you may at first need than to have a reprint in a few weeks' or months' time

■ the type of finish – loose-leaf ringbinders, spiral bound, saddle-stitched, etc (again, the printer can advise you here)

■ how the materials will be distributed.

Paper

Another significant choice to make is the type of paper. Paper has a number of characteristics that you need to be aware of, such as colour (a variety of colours and shades are available); grain (the direction in which the fibre in the paper lies); and weight (measured in grammes per square meter – see below).

There are many paper types, some of the most common being cartridge (tough and opaque); bond (crisp, tough paper with a matt surface); letterhead or stationery paper; and art paper (coated with china clay and specially treated to give it a very high smoothness and gloss).

Size

There are International ISO (International Standards Organisation) paper sizes used by paper manufacturers. The largest trimmed sheet size is A0 (measuring one square meter); the sizes go down to A10 (26 x 37mm). Each size is derived by halving the size immediately above it, so A1 is half of A0, A2 is half of A1, and so on. The most commonly used are A4 and A5. There are also standard book sizes. In the UK these include, for example, Demy Octavo and Royal Octavo (which measures 234 x 156mm, and in which size this book is printed).

When selecting paper size, check with your printer what is economical to put on the press, because this reduces wastage and therefore saves money.

Weight

Paper weights are measured in grammes per square meter (gsm or g/m^2). This book, for example, is printed on 90 gsm paper.

In brief

- Materials should be clean and clear, have a pleasing layout, use appropriate colours and illustrations, promote a desire to learn, and create an image of professionalism.

- When deciding on the format you should consider your purpose and your materials' relevance, proportion, direction, consistency, contrast, and simplicity. Attention to detail pays off.

- There are many ways in which you can present your information more attractively, eg through a well-judged use of bullet points, typography, white space, borders and boxes.

- Paragraphs, spacing, and indents should be consistent throughout your materials.

- Draw up with the printer a clear specification of your requirements for the finished product.

4

Introduction to Open Learning

Organisations in the 1990s are having to respond in a fast, flexible, and cost-effective way to meet changes in new market demands, technology, organisational structures, working methods, and procedures. As a result, all staff need to gain high levels of skills and knowledge. Given the scale and urgency of today's needs, some organisations are finding drawbacks in using conventional training methods and have been looking at new ones.

Conventional training still plays an important role in communicating knowledge and skills at key times in a person's career. Courses alone, however, will not meet the volume and variety of training needs that we face now and in the future. A more flexible, accessible, cost-effective, and relevant training method is needed. Open learning is one such.

In this chapter I discuss what open learning is, its advantages, limitations, and the benefits, and give guidelines on developing text-based materials. (TBT is covered in Chapter 5.)

What is open learning?

The term 'open learning' describes a learner-centred programme of training; 'learner-centred' means that it is flexibly designed to meet individual needs. It enables learners to study at a time, place, and pace convenient to them and to their employer.

How does open learning differ from conventional training?

In conventional training, people are taught the required skills and knowledge by a specialist in the subject. Open learning takes a different approach. It puts the content of the training session into a self-instructional format which is interactive, and so involves the learner throughout.

This type of learner-centred training offers both individuals and organisations a flexibility over what, when, where, and how training takes place. For individuals, it offers choice and encourages them to take on more responsibility for their own development. For organisations, a flexible training method can overcome some of the barriers of conventional training. It can be cost-effective and foster a learning culture within the organisation, rather than a culture where training and actual work are seen as separate. Furthermore, large numbers can be trained quickly and effectively. (The main differences between conventional training and open learning are summarised in Table 7 opposite.)

Giving learners more choice does not mean they make *all* the choices. It does however allow individuals to decide with their trainer or manager how 'open' the training should be, freeing themselves from the limitations of a more conventional approach.

Although I have said that learners decide what, when, where, and how they study, in reality the extent to which their training is 'open' or 'closed' depends on the discussion with their trainer or manager, or on which training approach has already been selected by their company for the open learning programme. For example, such a programme could involve learners' using text-based materials:

∎ on their own at a time agreed with their line manager or supervisor, perhaps with support such as a tutor or workshop

Table 7

CONVENTIONAL TRAINING vs OPEN LEARNING

	Conventional training	Open learning
Who	Attendance is often restricted by conditions or entry qualifications. This closes learning off from certain people.	Open learning often dispenses with prerequisites (eg experience, qualifications). It allows individuals to gain access to training where previously it has been unavailable or difficult to attend (eg for shift or evening workers, part-timers).
When	Training occurs at a predetermined time and place. This often involves time off work, and travel. The continuity of training can at times be interrupted owing to work pressures. The pace is normally geared to the 'average' trainee. This may cause difficulties – the slower learner may find it difficult to keep up, whereas the quick learner may be bored.	Learners can decide what time they study – at home, in lunch breaks, while commuting. Open learning is flexible and so can be adapted to allow for unforeseen circumstances such as work deadlines, holidays, and sickness.
What	Once a course is chosen, the precise topic is restricted. This can cause difficulties in meeting individual needs.	The subject and content of the training is selected by the learner (normally in consultation with their trainer or manager). Training can therefore be tailored to meet individual needs.
How	Because the training methods, resources, and type of assessment are decided by the trainer, learners are given no choice as to how they learn.	Individuals can study in the way that suits them best. The final choice of media, though, should take into account organisational needs, the resources available, and the cost.

■ in group sessions under the guidance and support of a trainer, eg for discussion exercises

■ with other media such as videos, CD-ROM, or CBT (computer-based training) in order to reinforce the main learning-points and provide real-life simulations.

In planning open learning you should decide quite how 'open' the training should be. This influences the type of training methods and materials you select.

Advantages and limitations of open learning formats

Open learning can be used in numerous situations. Text-based materials can be useful when training people in first principles, or providing basic knowledge for a qualification, for example. As a training method it has proved to have many benefits for a variety of organisations, helping them to improve performance, increase profitability, and enhance job satisfaction.

There are a number of formats on the market, all of which have their advantages and limitations. When considering different options with learners, to see which meet their needs best I find it helpful to refer to a check-list similar to the one in Table 8 on pages 61–63. (See also Table 5 on page 20.)

Table 8

ADVANTAGES AND LIMITATIONS OF OPEN LEARNING

Medium	Advantages	Limitations
Audiocassettes	▪ Easy to use. ▪ Can be listened to at a time, place, and pace convenient to the individual. ▪ Can be widely distributed. ▪ Useful when other forms of training input are impossible to use. ▪ Flexible – learners can stop, start, and replay the tape at will. ▪ Relatively cheap. ▪ Low-cost equipment. ▪ Do not date so quickly as video.	▪ Can be expensive to change. ▪ Students need access to equipment. ▪ Not very interactive. ▪ Learners can be reluctant to listen. ▪ Sophisticated recordings need to be produced professionally, which can be expensive.
CBT (computer-based training)	▪ Flexible and easy to use. ▪ Cost-effective. ▪ Convenient. ▪ Can be widely distributed and used again. ▪ Learner-paced. ▪ Consistent approach to training for each learner. ▪ Individualised feedback. ▪ Software is cheap. ▪ Wide choice of packages.	▪ In some cases there is no immediate record of a learner's work. A few producers do, however, now include reporting systems in their packages. ▪ Lacks personal contact. ▪ Can be expensive to update.
Interactive Video (IV), CD-ROM and CD-i	▪ Cost-effective (especially if large numbers need to be trained). ▪ Flexible and easy to use. ▪ Training can be individualised. ▪ Learner-paced. ▪ Learners forced to be fully involved.	▪ Development and production can be lengthy and costs high. ▪ Programs may not be completely relevant.

continued on page 62

Table 8 (continued)

ADVANTAGES AND LIMITATIONS OF OPEN LEARNING

Medium	Advantages	Limitations
Interactive Video (IV), CD-ROM and CD-i *(cont)*	■ Motivating and fast-moving. ■ Learners receive rapid feedback. ■ Monitors and records learners' progress. ■ Training packages are reusable. ■ IV and CD-i have high-quality video. ■ Wide selection of off-the-shelf courses for IV; choice of CD-ROM & CD-i packages is rapidly expanding. ■ Some packages can be customised. ■ CDs offer portable and convenient storage, cutting down on distribution cost; also easier to install than floppy disks.	■ With CD-ROM there may be problems with compatibility and formatting, depending on the software and equipment used. ■ Student-tracking systems are unlikely to be available on CD-i, unless it is linked to a computer.
Text-based materials	■ Cost-effective. ■ Flexible and portable. ■ Relatively cheap to produce and update. ■ Easy to use. ■ Provides a record of learners' responses.	■ Needs to be professionally produced if you are going to sell it, but can also be produced in-house. ■ Not as interactive as TBT materials and may need support, particularly if practical skills are involved.
The Internet	■ Provision of on-line self-paced learning across a world-wide network. ■ On-line support (usually through a keyboard). ■ Contact with other learners. ■ Sharing of common information.	■ Technology is not yet easily accessible.

continued opposite

Table 8 (continued)

ADVANTAGES AND LIMITATIONS OF OPEN LEARNING

Medium	Advantages	Limitations
The Internet *(cont)*	▌ Information is up to date. ▌ Easy to update. ▌ Relatively inexpensive.	
Video	▌ Convenient, flexible, and low-cost. ▌ Portable. ▌ Useful for portraying real-life situations. ▌ Stimulates trainees to ask questions and to test out new approaches in the workplace. ▌ Provides a high-impact, high-interest learning experience. ▌ Relatively long shelf-life. ▌ Learners can stop and review. ▌ Wide choice.	▌ Expensive to update. ▌ Off-the-shelf videos may not be entirely relevant. ▌ Must be professionally produced. ▌ Realism may be lacking. ▌ Trainees need access to specialist equipment. ▌ Passive medium. ▌ Can appear old-fashioned: the content is still good but the actors' clothes date it (eg flared trousers...).
Video-conferencing	▌ Access to multi-sited locations world-wide. ▌ Face-to-face support and contact with fellow learners and tutors.	▌ Can be costly in terms of equipment. ▌ Technology not very accessible.

Elements of an open learning programme

All open learning programmes should consist of two elements: support systems and learning materials.

Support systems

Before selecting materials, you should consider what type of support you can provide. Leaving people to study on their own can have detrimental effects. Some learners have the discipline and motivation to complete self-study courses; others may find it difficult, especially if a problem arises and there is no one to turn to. To be effective, open learning needs such support systems as:

- tutorials
- coaching
- mentoring schemes
- review sessions
- telephone tutorials
- telephone/fax help-lines
- self-help groups
- work-based activities
- practical exercises
- project work
- assessments.

Learning materials

Open learning materials are often referred to as a 'package' – an all-encompassing term that gives little idea as to what they consist of. In reality, a 'package' can consist of one or more media. It can be a single workbook; a video/audio cassette; a CBT, CD-ROM, or CD-i multimedia package; or a combination of these. Text-based materials are still the most commonly used form of open learning because they are relatively cheap to produce.

Because of the lack of personal contact in self-study materials, designers should pay special attention to detail. They should involve learners throughout, to catch their attention and guide them through the course. Some key features of open learning materials are:

- clear objectives
- self-instructional text
- clear headings
- activities and feedback

∎ self-assessment questionnaires and answers

∎ clear and attractive layout

∎ summaries and tips.

Open learning materials tend to fall within two broad categories – text-based materials and technology-based materials. The term TBT (technology-based training) refers to a number of applications of technology to training, such as CBT, CD-ROM, CD-i, and IV. These are discussed in Chapter 5.

Development options: text-based open learning materials

Many of the points mentioned in the preceding chapters are applicable to text-based open learning. When developing text-based open learning materials, there is a number of options: to use existing generic materials, to customise them, or to develop a bespoke product. (See also the previous discussion on pages 17 – 19.)

Generic materials

There is a wide range of generic materials on the market produced by companies such as the National Extension College, the Open College, and the Open University. They cover subject areas such as management, training and development, assessor training, health care, finance, sales, and electronics. Some provide the requisite knowledge for courses leading to qualifications.

Customising materials

If generic materials (in-house or external) do not meet your precise needs, you may want to consider developing an additional module, which may provide examples and exercises based on your organisational needs. You might also customise the actual text to meet your needs, eg by including industry-specific examples.

Bespoke

The development time and costs involved in developing a bespoke product depend on many variables, such as whether it is being produced in-house or externally, the length of module, and the nature of the materials.

Developing the materials
Planning

When planning text-based open learning materials (see Chapter 1), estimate carefully at the planning stage how long it will take to develop and produce the product. It is easy to underestimate how much time you will need. Some salutary remarks from those with experience may be helpful in order to drive this point home. The first caution comes from Christopher Brookes, international director of the Open College.

> To develop and produce an average text-based open learning module of 70 to 100 pages will take 10 to 12 weeks to camera-ready copy; then there is printing on top. It is essential to build in sufficient time for this part of the process at the planning stage. As a guideline, to run 500 copies of two modules (of 70 to 100 pages each) would probably take a further two or three weeks. This means a project of this size could take three to four months to complete. If other media, such as video or audio, or a greater number of modules are included in the programme it could take longer.

According to Roger Merritt, assistant director of the National Extension College, the budget has to be scrutinised as carefully as the schedule:

> Developing open learning materials is never as easy or as cheap as you think. Anyone thinking of developing open learning materials should remember that you do not just produce the materials once. It is a constantly evolving process and does not stop on publication. Whether you are developing a product for skills, knowledge, or for a qualification there will

be times when you may need to revise or update them. This should be taken into account when budgeting.

Design and development

When you are developing a product, a specification should be drawn up of your requirements along with a project plan (see Chapter 1). With these to hand the programme can be sourced and writing begin. Background research should include existing sources of materials, because some may be suitable for adaptation to an open learning format. Look at:

- materials you have already developed for conventional courses. You may be able to use the complete programme or perhaps just some of the activities as a basis for self-assessment questions.
- case-studies. Usually the basis already for learner activity, these are an essential part of flexible learning.
- your own course notes. They may cover content that your learners need, and already be in a concise form.
- text-book extracts. If used, they should be cleared for copyright. Alternatively, you could simply refer to them.
- internal manuals. These may already go some way towards being interactive material. Extracts can be used without copyright difficulties.
- worksheets and assignments.
- problems and projects.

Following the research it is advisable to set quality criteria (see page 19) before detailed design starts. The effectiveness of the materials can then be measured and signed off against them.

It you are working on a large project you will need to involve several writers, each being assigned a subject area or certain modules to develop. A managing editor will be responsible for ensuring that the writing is consistent with both the subject and style specification (eg in-house design and presentation styles), and that it meets the standards set. Once the writing is complete the technical editing takes over in order to produce clean texts.

Let us turn to the most pressing matters that the designer has now to consider.

Objectives

As I have stressed before, you must be absolutely clear about what you want to achieve.

Structure

The structure of a programme affects how well learners transfer new knowledge from the course to the job. A modular structure is more useful than a single block of training, because it enables information to be put into more manageable chunks. Clarity is in any case the key word here: people must be able to find information relevant to them as easily as possible.

Access devices

These are simply intended to help readers find their way around the course and get the most out of it. They include standard items such as a thorough contents list and a helpful index; a well-written introduction; 'project plans' (see page 26) to show how modules are linked and which ones may be appropriate; and 'icons' (pictorial devices) in the margin or by the running head to highlight activities, check-lists and other material. Let us look at one access device, the introduction, in a bit more detail.

Introduction

Both learners and those providing support (eg line managers and trainers) should be provided with a clear introduction to the materials. This could be a briefing session before the course or in written form. Either way, what do you need to include?

Your introduction might include:

∎ guidelines for readers on how to use the materials and plan their learning

- information on where this module fits into the overall programme
- course objectives and structure
- instructions on how to complete activities and assignments and on how feedback is provided
- any pre-required knowledge
- a description of how the course relates to certain qualifications (such as NVQs)
- assessment
- guidance on what support is available
- information on other packages in the series.

Other support material

Consideration needs to be given to the development of any support materials (eg audiocassettes and videos). These may be an integral part of the learning process itself, perhaps as part of a case-study, and are normally developed in tandem with the overall learning materials.

Activities and feedback

It is essential for learners to have the opportunity to try out their newly acquired knowledge; in other words, they need learning activities. When writing activities for open learning (including TBT), you should follow four basic principles:

1 Build opportunities into the programme for learners to *test* their knowledge or skills – for example, through questions and problems.

2 Enable learners to progress through the training by *achieving*. Repeated failure is disheartening. The designer, therefore, must pose problems that make learners think but are not impossible to solve. This way learners get a feeling of achievement. On completion, feedback is given on how they have performed – did they answer the questions correctly?

3   Provide positive feedback. Explaining to learners where they went wrong and encouraging them to try again is at the heart of good teaching. (Providing feedback that simulates the type a tutor may give face-to-face is a particular strength of TBT.) With text-based open learning materials, the best way of providing feedback is through written comments and support systems (eg reviews with a tutor or workshops), which provide learners with an opportunity to discuss any concerns they may have.

4   Make the programme as 'learner-centred' as possible and create two-way communication. This effect can be achieved in all types of open learning materials by having a group of learners in mind and using language and a style acceptable to them. (For instance, TBT is developed in a way that creates a feeling that the computer is talking to the user.)

At times learners may be tempted to miss activities. You cannot prevent this, but you can try to encourage people to complete them by:

■   making them relevant
■   giving a clear idea of what each is about and how learners will benefit from doing them
■   using activities as part of group work
■   reviewing activities with a tutor as part of the course
■   providing variety.

Type of activities

You can get learners involved quite easily by:

■   using pre- and post-course tests to test knowledge, understanding, and skills
■   regularly including exercises and questions in the body of the materials
■   setting self-tests, eg a set of questions at the end of each module to check understanding

▐ setting assignments.

Activities can be developed in various ways. In printed materials, learners may be asked to fill the blanks in sentences (with answers put at the end of the workbook); arrange information in the right order; or provide definitions of certain terms (such as 'multimedia'). Figure 16 is an activity from 'Managing Employee Relations', one of the modules in the Open College's New Supervision series. Learners are asked to draw on their own experiences and, on completing the activity, to check the comments at the end of the workbook (see Figure 17 on page 72) and also to complete the 'informal solutions check-list' in the workbook 'action chart'.

Figure 16

ACTIVITY FROM 'HOW TO HANDLE A DISCIPLINARY ISSUE'

ACTIVITY 7

Think of three recent incidents when informal disciplinary action was taken in your department. Write them down in the left-hand column below.

Then put the action that was taken in the middle column.

Finally, think about whether another solution would have been better in each case. If so, note what action would have been more appropriate in the right-hand column.

Incident	Action taken	Alternative action which might have been better.
1.		
2.		
3.		

Figure 17

COMMENTS ON ACTIVITY 7

Possible alternative ways of dealing with a disciplinary issue formally include:

- Moving to another job
- Enforcing rules more strictly
- Retraining
- Counselling
- Informal reprimand
- Making instructions clearer
- Using discussion to solve a conflict between team members
- Renegotiating the rule with your manager
- Getting the whole team together to solve the problem
- Encouraging the disciplinee not to let the team down
- Setting up an incentive scheme
- Explaining the reason for the rule
- Setting a good example.

The 'informal solution' includes a number of questions relating to this activity:

- Do you keep an eye open for trouble so that you can stop it developing into something serious?
- When counselling someone, do you remember to let them do 90 per cent of the talking?
- Do you encourage the person to find his or her own solution?
- Have you made it easy to identify potential problems by setting acceptable standards of conduct against which you can compare each team member's behaviour?

Assignments

Assignments are often in the form of printed materials, and need to be assessed by a tutor who can provide guidance on completing them. They are designed to give learners feedback on how they are progressing, and they also provide people with an opportunity to apply what they have learnt to their own situation. Quite a bit of practical or project work may be involved. For example, an assignment may involve:

■ learners' own work situations, eg describing the implementation of a new procedure

■ a case-study of a company, eg compiling a report on how someone dealt with a given problem.

Accompanying any assignment should be learner guidelines on: the aims; how long it should take; how to go about writing the report; and what the tutor will be looking for, eg evidence that you can apply some of the main ideas from the course to the case-study. Where long assignments are involved (say, 40 to 60 hours' work), guidance may also be given on scheduling and drawing up a study plan. A typical study plan might look like the one in Figure 18.

Figure 18

STUDY PLAN

Stages	Time guidelines	Target date	Revised date
Set and agree terms of reference	Within first two weeks	10 May 1996	
Identify and plan what information is required for the project	Third week	17 May 1996	
Research, gather, and collate the information	By end of sixth or seventh week	14 June 1996	21 June 1996

Checking and reviewing

An important part of any training is to check understanding. With text-based open learning, there are different ways in which both during and after training you can help learners check and review what they have learnt. The designer can build in different types of activities to be discussed between learners and their managers, mentor, or tutor. Students may be asked to:

- reflect on what they have achieved as a result of working through a module – has their performance improved, are there ideas they would like to develop further? The answers can then be reviewed with the appropriate manager or with the tutor.

- answer a questionnaire asking them, for instance, to list seven steps to successful problem-solving (with the answers provided at the end of the workbook).

Action plans

To help learners apply what they have learnt to their own work situations, a technique that some designers use is to include a learning diary or action plan. A learning diary records significant learning-points, reactions to the learning, and notes on how it can be applied. An example of a typical learning diary can be seen in Figure 19.

Figure 19

LEARNING DIARY

Topic	Learning-points	Reactions to learning	How can I apply the learning?

Action plans aim to get learners to assess where they are now in their job, where they want to be, and how to go about getting there. Designers sometimes include action plans, to be completed as students work through the course. This will probably involve them in gathering further information and discussing points with their manager, colleagues, or others.

In brief

- ▌ Open learning is a learner-centred programme of training that allows learners to choose what, how, when, and where they study.

- ▌ The difference between conventional training and open learning is that, in the former, learners are taught the skills and knowledge they need by a trainer; open learning uses a self-instructional format which is interactive and keeps learners involved.

- ▌ Open learning materials fall into two broad categories: text-based open learning and technology-based training (TBT). They offer many benefits, such as being flexible, interactive, and easy to use.

- ▌ Learner involvement can be achieved by including activities, pre- and post-course tests, self-tests, and assignments.

- ▌ Feedback should acknowledge learners' efforts, give reassurance, indicate strengths and weaknesses, and provide advice on how to improve weaker areas.

- ▌ It is a fundamental mission of open learning to provide adequate support to learners while assisting them to become more independent and take more control over their learning.

5

Technology-based Training (TBT)

The word *technology* tends to create excitement or fear depending on how computer-literate you are. Come what may, though, technology is here to stay. As multimedia has become easier to use and more affordable, companies are turning to computer-based 'interactive multimedia' in such areas as training, presentations, and sales.

Here I discuss what TBT is; its applications; equipment requirements; and how to develop TBT programs. Audiovisual aids are also discussed.

What is TBT and 'interactive multimedia'?

The term TBT (technology-based training) refers to a number of applications of technology to training, such as Computer-based Training (CBT), Compact Disk-Read Only Memory (CD-ROM), Compact Disk interactive (CD-i), Interactive Video (IV), the Internet, and video-conferencing.

Interactive multimedia refers to combinations of different media along with the opportunity for learners to interact with them.

To make the information both interesting and accessible to a wide audience, most multimedia programs use interactivity, which allows learners to review and study the data, ask and answer questions, make choices and decisions, experiment with a range of options, and carry out a variety of activities and tests to check their understanding. By building an element of 'doing' – interactivity – into a learning programme, it is possible to raise retention levels to about 70 per cent of the material, more than twice the retention rate for those who simply see and hear what they need to learn. Interaction is crucial to effective learning and communications applications. It may involve users in different ways – by asking them to click on buttons and menu options, type in answers to questions, or use the mouse to drag objects across the screen. To illustrate how a learner might interact with a package, I have included a couple of screen shots from one of Xebec's training programs (Figures 20 and 21).

Figure 20

IN THE OFFICE (1)

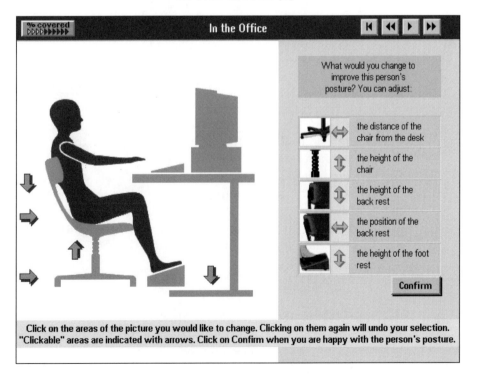

Figure 21

IN THE OFFICE (2)

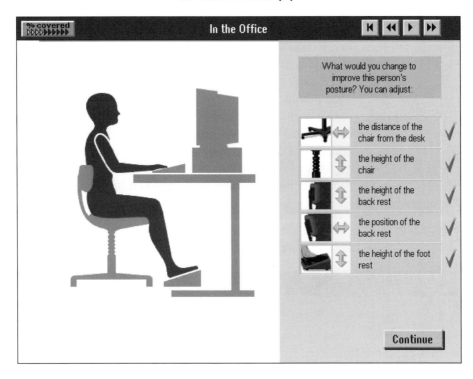

In Figure 20 the user is asked to improve the person's sitting position by clicking and dragging objects. When the user is happy with the result he or she confirms the answer by clicking on 'Confirm'. In Figure 21 the screen shows the user how he or she has done by indicating against the different positions which are correct (by showing a tick) and which incorrect (by showing a cross).

These are the media that lend themselves to interactive multimedia:

Text   Printed materials can, as we have seen, be manipulated in a variety of ways to increase interactivity.

Audio The use of sound eg a keynote speech from the chairman of the company (the human voice), or music and sound effects. TBT packages are often audio-driven – the audio becomes the tutor.

Graphics Graphics can be inserted into a programme using techniques such as scanning or by importing them from clipart, eg company logos, drawings, diagrams, paintings, maps, charts, computer graphics, and cartoons.

Still pictures Photographs or video stills can be used. For example, you could use a series of photographs to show someone how to assemble a piece of equipment, or have photographs of the chief executive and senior managers within a company for a 'who's who' section in a document.

Animation Computer-generated images can produce apparently three-dimensional figures, such as the metamorphosis of a butterfly, or a plant growing.

Video This is highly adaptable and can be used in a variety of ways, eg to highlight key learning-points, to show different behaviours, to capture role-plays, or to depict hazardous situations.

TBT formats

There are a growing number of TBT formats now available. Some of the most commonly used are CBT, CD-ROM, CD-i, and IV. However, as technology improves and costs come down, interest is growing in using the Internet, satellite, and video-conferencing for training delivery.

CBT

CBT is the traditional way of developing interactive training and has been around for many years. It is largely a technology-driven medium which is limited by what the technology allows you to do. Some of the early programs were little more than page-turning devices. Today, however, with high-resolution graphics, it is possible to create moving images, speech, colour, and other different presentations to make materials more interactive and interesting.

Expert systems (knowledge-based systems) and artificial intelligence (a series of techniques that allow you to use the computer in a more flexible and versatile way) are being used in CBT and multimedia generally to simulate how a tutor would respond to a learner face to face, eg how a tutor would draw inferences about the learner's knowledge and understanding, decide what he or she is going to talk about next, and how to present the information. Such systems allow a genuine exchange of ideas, information, and analysis between the computer and the user.

The role of CBT is to use a tutorial style approach to solve training problems. By this I mean that the computer has a dialogue with the learner and allows him or her to interact with the program by using the keyboard or mouse to respond to activities or questions. The computer then assesses the responses and provides feedback before moving on and providing additional information; and so the process continues. Learners move throughout the course either in a linear sequence of tutorial frames or by branching around the program. The actual route taken depends on how they respond to activities and how well they perform.

With the rapid growth of computers, CBT is probably one of the most widely used TBT formats. There are many titles to choose from, easily distributed on 3½-inch floppy disks (although some 5¼-inch floppy disks are still around). Programs can either be loaded onto a hard disk or a computer network.

CD-ROM and CD-i

There are a growing number of high-quality generic packages now available on CD-ROM and CD-i, covering such subject areas as management skills, communications, finance, induction, health and safety, and personal computer training. As more producers/publishers get into this market, and as the technology improves for converting traditional media (eg going from video and audio to digital formats), so the choice will increase. Some of the leading producer/publishers for CD-ROM courses are Tarragon, Training Direct, and Xebec. The BBC, Melrose, and others are also moving into this market. The main producer/ publishers of CD-i are Melrose, Video Arts, and Phillips.

CD-ROM is delivered on a personal computer in the form of a CD disk or on the hard disk. To retrieve and manipulate the data, you access it through a CD-ROM drive, which is either an integral part of the computer or connected to it. CD-i is delivered through a CD-i player (similar to a videoplayer) linked to a TV monitor. A simple hand-held remote console unit (comprising of a joystick or mouse and several directional touch keys) is used to move through the material at a pace that suits the user.

To support multimedia, you need to have large storage capacity, a high-resolution colour screen, and a data-processing capability to store, retrieve, and manipulate the data at high speeds while providing a responsive, flexible, and reliable system. CDs (which typically hold at least 650MB of data in a read-only format) offer one solution. High volumes of computer data can be stored, captured, and manipulated in this way. For example, some of the most publicised CD-ROM packages on the home-market 'multimedia encyclopaedias' can hold around nine million words (the equivalent of a 27-volume paper-based encyclopaedia), and include on average 15 hours of audio,

8,000 pictures, and 100 video clips, all on one disk.

The advantage that CDs have over conventional magnetic media are that they are compact, portable, and more resistant to accidental damage and routine wear-and-tear than a 3½-inch disk. They are also more efficient in terms of speed and the volume and quality of data captured, stored, transmitted, and reproduced. The immediate advantages to developers are that CDs are cheaper to produce and harder to copy than a 3½-inch disk.

When converting video and film to a digital system, a large amount of storage and processing capacity are required, owing to the high-quality detail and colour of the originals. This can be done by compressing the amount of data to the minimum required for your program and by building into the program a routine that reconstructs the compressed information on demand.

To run full-motion video you need a multimedia PC (MPC) with a high specification (see page 91). Conventional video comprises a mass of still images which, when projected at a rate of 25 to 30 frames per second (fps), create an illusion of movement. You may have noticed that in some of the early CD-ROM packages video images appeared jerky. This is because the images are being played back at fewer than 25 to 30 fps. The international standard for compression systems is MPEG (Motion Picture Expert Group); if an MPEG card is included in a machine, the video quality can be improved significantly.

To summarise, therefore, the main strengths of CD-ROM and CD-i are:

Ease of use   Both CD-ROM and CD-i are easy to use. However, many people are more used to using a videoplayer than a computer and so many feel more comfortable with CD-i – all you have to do is plug in and play.

Variety of media Combining different forms of information in an inter-active way allows learners to explore subjects by a number of pathways, thus broadening the learning experience. Although training is normally a linear pathway, CD-ROM and CD-i allow learners to branch out at any point and explore information in greater depth.

Storage

CD-ROM and CD-i can store and read large quantities of information. With CD-ROM the PC stores, manipulates, and presents the information, whereas CD-i uses a videoplayer, hand control, and a TV monitor.

Interactive approach

Both formats offer interactive training. Flexible access and free movement around the program help users to build on their knowledge and test ideas through activities, quizzes, and drills. They can then apply that knowledge in a logical and meaningful way. CD-ROM tends to be slightly more interactive than CD-i because of the links with the computer and the ability to use a keyboard.

Learner independence

As training is 'learner-paced' users can work through the program independently, tailoring it to meet their needs and so concentrating on those elements or modules relevant to them.

Content

Courses are split into manageable chunks with pre-determined links.

Flexibility

With their modular structure, programs can be accessed in a flexible way through the use of on-screen navigational buttons.

Self-assessment facilities

These allow learners to monitor their progress and highlight areas where they may be having difficulties. Self-assessment, and receiving feedback, can take different forms. There are, for example, opportunities to practise and test understanding through activities, questionnaires, role-plays, and simulations. Feedback can be on-screen responses to 'what-if' questions through the use of case-studies, role-plays, and simulations. For example, you could show health and safety procedures for handling dangerous chemicals followed by the consequences of not following them correctly.

Help and guidance

Assistance is continually available in the form of on-screen navigational buttons, help tools, indexes, glossaries, and dictionaries.

Monitoring learners' progress

CD-ROM can monitor learners' progress through a built-in student tracking system. CD-i is unlikely to have this facility, unless it is a program linked to a computer.

All these strengths and benefits mean a cost-effective learning method that can lead to substantial long-term savings.

IV

IV, or interactive video, is a well-established training format. A wide range of high-quality generic materials is available, dealing with such areas as communicating effectively with customers or staff, appraisal, interviewing, teambuilding, customer care, and telephone techniques. A typical IV system (which is stored on a 12-inch laser disk) combines the naturalism and involvement of 'real' video with the flexibility and personalised learning routes throughout the material that computer software can provide.

A typical approach, for instance, might be to show a video-sequence of a receptionist having a chat on the phone to a friend. A customer arrives, but, instead of finishing the telephone call and dealing with the customer, the receptionist goes on talking. The video sequence stops at this point, and the user is asked how he or she thought the receptionist should have responded. The user is shown the consequences of the response through a further video-sequence. Successive attempts are allowed, so the user can compare the different responses.

With this method trainers can oversee learners' progress by using the computer to record the sequence that each learner follows, the standard of their answers, the results, and the time taken to complete different parts of the course. This allows them to highlight potential problem areas and to offer learners appropriate support.

The main limitations of IV are the high set-up costs (in terms of equipment) and the development costs. Rapid developments in CD technology could eventually mean that IV will be phased out as a training option.

Video CD

Video CD is becoming more accessible and is a good format for showing full-screen 'real' video requiring little interactivity, such as lectures. The main strengths of Video CD are that high-quality sound and video can be stored on it, and that users have more control over the program. It allows flexible and easy access to any part of the program through chapters and topics. For the trainer, it offers greater flexibility in how they use and access a video, and speeds up the finding of relevant sequences.

The Internet

Many of you will have heard of the Internet, but what can it offer you as trainers? The Internet is a network of computers that enables users to communicate world-wide through phone lines. As long as the computers are linked to the Internet, they can receive and transmit any programmed information, be it text, graphics, or sound.

There is a growing number of corporations looking to connect their own networks to an outside system such as the Internet and to have some kind of on-line presence in the form of, say, an e-mail account or a web page (a page could, for example, contain information on a company's products and services).

As part of the constant search for more innovative and creative ways of delivering training, the Internet is offering new opportunities. Support for self-paced courses can now be delivered on it; they can easily be maintained by an on-line tutor. On-line support allows communication between tutor and learner, or between students, by using the conventional e-mail facilities. If video-conferencing was also linked to the Internet, then simulated face-to-face communication would also be possible.

Potential benefits from using the Internet are that:

▌ it provides an easily accessible worldwide computer network

▌ information is up to date

▌ learning materials can be quickly updated

▌ there is access to multi-sited locations world-wide

▌ it offers trainers an additional cost-effective way of training staff, particularly those at remote sites or those who simply find it difficult to attend a course.

The Internet combines the flexibility and advantages of TBT self-paced learning with the interaction and motivation, in the form of on-line support, of classroom training. It is also relatively inexpensive. As video-conferencing becomes more accessible and prices come down, we may see more face-to-face support, too.

To use the Internet you need a computer, modem, and a telephone line. When selecting a modem consider how much information you are going to be sending. If your usage is going to be high it is advisable to consider a sophisticated modem that will increase the speed of receiving and transmitting data.

Satellite training

Long-distance interactive training by satellite allows direct access to a tutor during the broadcast via a phone link direct to the studio. The training is 'live', and people interested in participating in satellite training can subscribe and join in various programmes. The main benefits of satellite training are that:

▌ it can reach many people simultaneously across a large area

▌ it allows a subject expert to reach many people at one time

▌ the interactive element of the telephone means that

learners on the system can exchange views with one another, contribute to the programme itself, and influence how the programme is developed.

If you are interested in satellite training, a good starting-point is to look at the subjects currently broadcast to see if you have a need in any of those areas. Become involved with that programme and see if this form of delivery mechanism is suitable for your needs. If it is, you may want to consider developing and producing your own in the future.

Video-conferencing

Video-conferencing has been around for some time, but has been seen as expensive, difficult to use, and of limited benefit. (It also had a poor image in terms of quality and speed, because many of the systems were studio-based.) Now cheaper alternatives are beginning to appear and video-conferencing equipment can now range from a fixed conference facility, with a standard PC plus built-in camera, and a video, to a portable system, all linked to a phone. The equipment lets users hold long-distance conversations face-to-face on the screen. As this technology becomes more accessible and cheaper, we may see it more closely linked to the Internet.

With growing numbers of staff no longer based at one specific location, the Internet and video-conferencing can provide such facilities as e-mail, voicemail, and faxback. Not only will these facilities help individuals keep in touch with their company, they will also provide opportunities for the delivery of training (with on-line support) to staff in remote locations, reducing the feeling of isolation that many home- or mobile (working away from the office) workers have.

Applications

TBT has a lot to offer trainers, but it should not be seen as a panacea. It should be seen as an additional element for the trainer's kit-bag when considering the most appropriate way of meeting training needs. So why should you use TBT?

You may be finding that:

■ you have a training need that cannot be met through conventional methods
■ it is costly to run conventional courses
■ your learners are geographically dispersed
■ it is difficult to keep up with demand
■ it is difficult to release staff
■ you have a large number of people who need to be trained quickly and consistently
■ there are too few learners to run a cost-effective conventional course.

With TBT so easy to use and affordable, its powerful capabilities mean that learners can work at their own pace, without supervision, and at a convenient time and location. Because packages are reusable, large numbers of learners can be trained to consistently high standards at relatively low costs. Furthermore, CD technology provides realistic simulations, diagnostics, and interactive exercises that motivate learners to experiment within the safety of the program before facing the 'real' world.

For relatively low costs, TBT can be an ideal tool for providing learners with a comprehensive introduction to:

■ keyboard skills
■ computer software (a word-processing, spreadsheet, or presentation software package)
■ 'soft skills' in areas where role-plays for practising knowledge and skills are required (eg management, finance, business, and personal skills)
■ processes and procedures
■ simulations involving, for instance, operating complex equipment, drills and practice, decision-making,

process modelling, and fault-finding.

■ product and service knowledge (eg for new as well as existing products or services, so staff can promote them to customers and gain competitive advantage)

■ updating/refresher training for staff.

Just to give an example of the penultimate bullet point, a financial company that was introducing new products needed to ensure that all their staff (2,500 people spread across 70 branches) were trained quickly and consistently in the new products. They decided that the only way to train that many people in a short time was to develop an interactive CBT course and put it on the network. This allowed them to take the training to the learners, thus reducing both time off work and certain training costs such as travel. Eventually all staff completed the training. The company found that CBT training on the network offered significant benefits: everyone was trained in a consistent way before the product launch, and the training could be monitored and managed centrally, while branch managers took day-to-day responsibility for the training.

Returning to TBT in general, by interacting with the computer, learners can quickly get an understanding of the basics of a given topic (eg management theory) before converting this knowledge into effective skills through more conventional techniques such as a workshop. For example, an 'effective interviewing' CBT self-study package alone is unlikely to convert learners into effective interviewers, but what it can do is provide them with the theory that will help them prepare for interviews. The actual interviewing skills can then be practised in a workshop.

Many organisations are now finding particularly that a combination of TBT and personal tuition (from, say, a mentor) ensures optimum use of the material. It also provides opportunities for learners to express concerns, address difficulties, ask questions, and receive feedback.

Integrating open learning and TBT with traditional training

Because TBT is flexible, offering the possibility of using modules or activities in any combination to suit specific developmental needs, it has potential applications for group or individual learning alongside more conventional training programmes. You may want to consider using TBT for:

■ pre- and post-course tests. I have used such tests for a word-processing package in order to help identify a learner's needs, to monitor their progress, and to assess any improvement in performance as a result of training.

■ course 'pre-work'. TBT can be used to provide learners with the basics of a subject before they attend a training course. This ensures that all learners start with a similar knowledge level, and that the content is designed and delivered at an appropriate level of complexity.

■ individual study during or after training to reinforce learning or for further study.

■ integrating material into a learning session, eg as a course assignment to reinforce key learning-points, or to stimulate discussion. CD-i offers a flexible way of using video in a group session and may be used as a tool to make the video become more 'real' and exciting for the otherwise passive viewer. The video capability of CD-i is an ideal way of getting people involved, of helping them to understand problems that confront them in the workplace.

■ adding variety to training methods. Such variety puts trainers in a better position to help individuals select the method best suited to meeting their needs and preferred learning styles.

Equipment requirements

When purchasing materials you should check the specification and the CD-ROM drive speed required. Most software on the market works on dual speed, but (some notably video-intensive ones) usually need double speed, or as fast as possible. Some packages now require at least a quad-speed CD-ROM drive.

Inside many packages there is a recommended hardware specification. This does not mean that the software will not work on a machine with a lower specification and speed drive; it does mean, however, that the performance will be adversely affected.

Many companies have PCs without multimedia functionality. Before deciding to purchase a multimedia PC, you should investigate the feasibility of upgrading your existing hardware: there are a number of upgrade kits available. The hardware standard for multimedia systems is defined by the Multimedia PC (MPC) established by the Multimedia PC Marketing Council.

With rapid developments in technology and software it is advisable, when selecting equipment, to purchase the best you can afford at the time, because it may not be long before it is out of date. This month's state-of-the-art equipment may not be next's. Bear in mind therefore that the specifications below are *guidelines* only. You should seek specific advice from your IT department or courseware provider on what type of equipment you need. This will reduce the chance of purchasing equipment that fails to meet your requirements.

Choosing your equipment

It is important to match equipment against the applications you want to use. There are several points to consider. First of all, what capabilities do you want the hardware to have, and therefore what operating systems will you need? The configuration of your hardware needs to meet your requirements. You should be aware that some packages run using certain MPEG cards only, so if you do not have the right one there will be a compatibility problem. If you are looking at hardware for an open-learning environment without multimedia capability (ie you just want to use CBT) then you will probably find a 486 computer adequate. However, it is advisable to take your future requirements into account, as more and more courses are becoming available on CD-ROM.

If you *do* want to run multimedia courses, you need a multimedia personal computer (MPC) with sufficient power and memory to cope with the large amounts of data a multimedia program holds, a soundboard, videoboard, speakers, a CD-ROM drive (with sufficient speed), and preferably an MPEG card (to improve video quality). Many developers are now recommending a Pentium machine as the minimum specification for running multimedia courses. MPC Level 111 is the current specification.

For CD-i you need a videoplayer, a television (preferably with a 15 to 20-inch screen), and a mouse. For IV the equipment needed is a computer, keyboard, videodisk player, TV monitor, and communication links between them all.

Other important considerations are what training format you will be using now and in the future (CBT or multimedia CD-ROM), and whether you have the skills and knowledge internally to set up and configure the machine, or whether you will need technical support from your supplier. (Some suppliers now offer technical support, so it is worth checking what support services are available before making your purchase.) Finally, to develop successful multimedia applications you need a computer with a high specification designed for authoring systems (see below).

Authoring systems

The cost of having bespoke products developed by external organisations can be prohibitive, and a lot of companies just do not have the budget to go out and commission applications. But now, with a multimedia authoring system (eg Authorware Professional and Multimedia Toolbook), companies are in a position to develop their own applications.

Authoring systems offer a higher level of interaction through the use of hyperlinks (which present information in the way that most people learn – by association). They allow the user to interact directly with the system, giving them more control over what is displayed and the sequence in which it is viewed. They have many 'real' applications in all areas of learning and communications, and tend to approach development in different ways. Let us take Authorware Professional and Multimedia Toolbook as examples.

■ Authorware takes an icon/flowchart approach. (You do not have to be a programmer to use it.) Icons are used for putting in text, graphics, video, erasing things on screen and building in interaction. They are dragged and dropped onto a flowline that links the icons together to create a linear or branching structure for the application. The flowchart enables you to see how the application pans through and works together.

■ Multimedia Toolbook is a page-based system. The author puts objects onto pages (eg text, graphics, pushbuttons, sound) and then links the pages together. A powerful scripting language (similar to a programming language) allows you to build in interactivity. Toolbook also offers hyperlinking.

Which authoring package you select depends to some extent on your personal preferences, any past experience you may have of development tools, your organisation's needs, the resources and skills you have internally, and the type of materials you want to develop. Other considerations are: ease of use, the approach to development, software facilities (eg create/edit text, graphics), the speed and responsiveness of the system, ease of updating, and available support.

Your budget should take into account the cost of the

authoring tool (which might range from £700 up to many thousands for one of the leading tools) and any additional costs such as the equipment for the authoring; additional software (such as Photo CD, sound editors, or a 3-D animation package); and runtime costs. If you are looking to distribute the program, there may also be royalty fees.

Development options

There are four main options for developing TBT. You can:

- use existing generic TBT materials
- personalise generic packages by including company-specific material either within the TBT package or in additional material such as a workbook
- customise an existing package
- develop a bespoke product.

Generic materials

Before you consider developing a bespoke product it is worth looking at generic, off-the-shelf packages. You may be able to meet all, or at least some, of your learners' needs with materials that already exist. This saves you time, effort, and money. There are a wide range of packages available on the market, as discussed earlier. If you would like some tips on how to select appropriate materials, you may find Table 5 useful (page 20).

Costs for TBT can range from as little as £30 to many thousands, depending on your requirements – the format to be used, the sophistication of the application, or the number of users. Whatever your needs, though, it is worth looking at the different purchasing options that suppliers offer and considering the cost benefits of each. Cost-effective ways of buying TBT include a corporate licence; multi-user, site, or network licences (for CBT); buying in bulk; or taking out a library or rental option. If you have a large training department or regular training needs then it is normally cheaper to purchase. Conversely, if you are unsure of what your exact needs are, or have a small number of people to train, a library option may be best initially. You can always purchase later if you find the package is being used more than you expected.

Personalising

Obviously, if a package meets all your needs, that is great. However, there may be occasions when, although it meets a large percentage of your needs, there are still one or two small areas that are not covered. For relatively little cost (when compared with that of developing a bespoke product), designers can personalise a TBT package by adding their own information or by including additional support materials such as a workbook, audio, or video. This approach can be a good way of testing whether multimedia is right for your organisation without investing in expensive developments. Remember, though, that if you want to change any of the producer's material (computerised, printed, or other) you should get copyright permission. (As I have already mentioned, this may be costly but is still cheaper than developing a bespoke product.)

Although in many cases you need to approach the producer if you wish to personalise a package, a growing number of producer/publishers such as Tarragon and Xebec offer an optional toolkit that allows trainers to personalise courses themselves in-house by adding, for instance, specific information such as a logo, mission statement, or policies and procedures.

There may be occasions when you need to carry out testing – perhaps to evaluate staff performance or to measure skills. Another example of how you can personalise courses is to generate your own computerised tests. There are a few packages on the market with different features to help you design, build, and present tests with multiple choice questions, some of which also come with a test administrator.

This is a relatively inexpensive way of tailoring a package to meet your needs. Licensing agreements and costs can vary, though, and it is worth seeing what is on offer before a final decision is made.

Customising

When generic packages meet your needs only in part, discuss these needs with the producer. They have specialist teams who can advise you and also have access to a library of existing materials that may, if customised, fit the bill.

The cost and time involved in customising a package will depend on the modifications you require and whether or not the work is carried out in-house or by an external producer. Changes to text may take just a few days, but major changes such as importing video, graphics, and diagrams obviously require much more time – and money.

Bespoke products

Bespoke courseware can be developed either in-house or by an external producer. Developing a bespoke product is costly and time-consuming, but there may be occasions when this is the only option available to you, especially if the subject you want to train people in is highly specific to your organisation.

Developing the program

Developing multimedia packages is a complex task and very much a collaborative effort, involving a production team of people from a variety of disciplines.

The first step in any project is to appoint a project manager to co-ordinate the whole development and production process. It is his or her responsibility to decide on a strategy, set up project management and reporting systems, get together a production team, train team members (if necessary), set quality standards, and ensure that time-scales are met and that the project remains within budget.

To make up a good production team, you need (depending on the type of program you are developing) people with:

■ subject expertise (best provided by the sponsor of the project)

■ training experience

■ instructional design experience

■ writing and editing skills

■ programming experience

■ experience of producing the media required (print, audio, video, CBT, CD-ROM, etc).

One of the most important ingredients is instructional design. This requires an understanding of how people learn and the ability to analyse and arrange information in a way that is meaningful and attractive to the intended audience.

Initial design
The proposal

When you approach a producer, the first step is to discuss your requirements in terms of objectives, the proposed target group, and the time-scale and budget, so that a proposal can be drawn up. Having an outline plan (see Chapter 1) before you speak to the producer reduces the amount of work needed to draw up a proposal. It also provides a firm basis on which to discuss your requirements ('what you are trying to achieve') with the producer.

Once the proposal has been agreed with the client, the outline design document is written up. This includes such things as top-level objectives, and how the main menu and subsequent sections will look. At this stage it is advisable to establish with the producer quality standards against which you can assess the effectiveness of the course. From here the detailed design work starts – to flesh out the content, decide what will be seen on screen (eg in terms of text, graphics, or video), choose the audio track script or video clips, and see how all the parts interrelate. In considering screen layout, the designer has to combine graphics, text, and colour in a structure that develops a dialogue with the learner. This can be in the form of information, questions, responses, and feedback. The result of this detailed work is then passed to the author, who will program the changes and provide prototypes for the client's approval.

Design features

Looking more specifically at the program content, good design principles help to smooth the learners' path. Clear and relevant features assist learners in finding their way around the program. A few examples of devices used in introductions and in the main part of the programs include:

I   a module with information on the course's structure and content, and on how to find your way around

I   menus and submenus

I   glossaries and indexes – typical searches might be for the meaning of words or topics

I   clear instructions on how to use the navigational buttons or icons within the program to move around the screens, and to find help facilities

I   pre-tests – eg in the case of a CBT package on wordprocessing software, questions on the different functions and capabilities of the package for the user to complete.

I   a toolbar (with the navigational buttons on) allowing the user to move easily around the screen and the course – eg, icons could be included to ease access to menus, modules, topics, summaries, and tests.

I   hotspots – in some programs a part of the screen is sensitised so that, if selected be clicking on the spot, it causes another action to occur. 'Hotspots' could be a word or part of a picture, hence by clicking on the word 'multimedia', for example, a window appears with further information about that topic. When the user has finished reading the description, he or she simply clicks on the screen again to return to the original screen.

Routing systems and flowcharts

A good designer will take advantage of one of the main benefits of TBT: the ability to build in a complex routing system generated by interaction. This produces two-way communication between the learner and the designer. For example, a learner may be asked to answer questions, complete an activity, and be provided with an opportunity to practise skills (eg, in the case of PC training, in a particular piece of software). The learner is then provided with feedback based on his or her responses.

The instructional designer may also be responsible for producing a graphic representation of the training program – a flowchart – specifying what will be seen on the screen (eg text, graphics, video, or audio tracks), when and where information should appear, and in what form. It is essentially a map through the information in the training program, showing how all the elements interrelate. This stage may also involve developing scripts, storyboarding (see pages 30–31), and designing any support materials such as text and audiocassettes.

The designer should ensure above all that the client sponsoring the program understands what the product will look like once complete.

Resources

The next stage is to develop the resources that make up part of the program – the video or audio tracks, graphics, and text-based materials. These are produced by specialist teams including graphic designers, writers, editors, and video producers. The programmers draw up a functional specification to suggest how the content can be translated into programming language and thus be presented on screen. Initially, the programmers may develop prototypes for the client to see and pass an opinion on.

At this stage there is also the whole question of screen format. A basic layout is decided on, with windows and boxes. Background and foreground colours are selected. A clear and helpful style is developed for the graphics – tables, for instance, so designed that the information in them can be readily understood. As for text, an appropriate typeface is chosen and set at a comfortable line-length; and such features as scrolling (vertically and horizontally) are built in. All this determines the basic look of the program. Figure 22, from a Xebec CD-ROM training package, shows one way to integrate some of these features.

Figure 22

EXAMPLE OF SCREEN FORMAT

When the resources have been made, the programmers then build the actual product by pulling in the graphics, video and audio tracks etc, and putting the text on the screen.

Testing and piloting

Testing and piloting are crucial to the success of a program. During development, testing is a continual process both internally and with the client against the agreed standards. This may involve the producer testing out ideas and screen layouts on the client, checking the content and agreeing a script, and making sure that the program hangs together in the right sequence. By checking things as they are designed or programmed, modifications can be made based on feedback, thus reducing the amount of testing needed at the pilot stage.

When development work has been completed, a Beta version is usually produced so that the course can be piloted by the client. The aim is to check that the program meets the objectives, is usable by the target audience, and that the whole course hangs together. If an administration or student-tracking system is included, this is also checked to verify that it does help measure learners' performance.

Modifications are made, if necessary, following feedback from the pilot. To make substantial changes at this stage involves extra work and more cost to the client; for this reason, it is worth holding back part of your budget for contingencies. When the client is happy with the product, it is signed off against the agreed quality standards and sent to production and then, finally, distribution.

Audiovisuals

Audiovisual includes audiocassettes and video. Let us look at each in turn.

Audiocassettes

Audiocassettes are a useful resource, because most people

have access to an audiotape player either at home or in the car. They are also cheap. They should not, though, be used simply for the sake of providing variety – there should be clear benefits to be had.

Cassettes are best used for training that involves verbal skills. The following are examples of how blank and generic audiocassette-based packages can be used:

- as part of a language course – to listen to either at home or in a language lab to help learners practise speaking a language and compare their responses and accents with those of native speakers
- in role-plays – blank audiotapes can be used to record a learner's performance in a role-play involving the telephone; as part of the feedback, the trainer plays the tape and asks the individual (and any others present) how he or she feels about their performance.
- as part of a self-paced study course to demonstrate sounds and include role-plays or expert speakers on particular topics
- for self-development.

Audiocassettes can also be used for briefing employees, introducing a topic, presenting new ideas, guiding learners through a hands-on task, influencing feelings and attitudes, and for revision and summary purposes. (See also Table 8, pages 61–63.)

It can be relatively cheap to produce audiocassettes. If you do decide to produce one, then you should bear in mind the following considerations:

Introduction   Learners need clear guidance on how to approach the training.

Access devices   To help listeners find their way around the tape, spoken section numbers could be included, together with clear written guidelines to be followed while the tape plays.

Tone of voice   It is important to maintain listeners' interest, so the tone of voice used should be informal and personal, as though the speaker were talking directly to whoever is listening. A low-pitched voice with little variation in tone is unlikely to catch people's attention.

Script

Keep straight talking to a minimum. Do not go on for a long time, unless you introduce other sounds or voices to keep up interest. For example, you might use two presenters or include pre-recorded interviews, or discussions with other people, eg other learners' experiences, managers' experiences etc.

Maintaining interest

To involve listeners more you can add variety by linking the audiocassette with other media. You could, for instance:

- ask learners to listen to a role-play on the tape before writing their observations in a workbook
- have learners listen to an extract on tape and then complete a written exercise before listening to the answers
- refer to photographs in a book so learners can visualise what is being discussed
- have learners in a language lab listen to the tutor and then repeat onto the tape what he or she has said, thus allowing learners to compare their pronunciation with the tutor's
- verbally guide learners through different tasks and activities or practical exercises involving a series of responses, eg operating a piece of software, or completing a form or questionnaire.

Support material

Even if the training package consists solely of an audio-cassette, you need some form of printed material to let learners know what they should be doing and how to get the most out of the package.

Video

Video (and film) is spectator-oriented: participants watch passively rather than getting involved. It is important, therefore, to try to get learners involved, and to build the video into the training session as a genuine learning aid, eg as part of a discussion exercise, or as something intended to demonstrate attitudes and behaviours.

Videos can be used to:

- provide insight into a situation that participants would otherwise not have seen (eg inside a nuclear reactor plant or a research laboratory)
- update employees on topics that are unlikely to change
- demonstrate and explain something vividly – make it feel 'real'
- assist self-study (eg developing PC skills)
- provide background information on a company
- illustrate key points from a training session
- to record (with blank tapes) role-plays and provide feedback on learners' performance.

Before a video is shown, participants should be briefed on what they are going to view and what they will be required to do as a result of watching it. For example, if you are showing a video on 'How to Manage Staff' you may ask the group for their comments on what happened in the video – what elements of bad management were demonstrated? Correct answers can be put up on a flipchart.

One of the limitations of video is that it can be difficult to access specific sequences quickly. In some video-based training packages, the self-study version of the video often has on-screen icons relating to specific modules or sections in a workbook (a complete course based around the video) to ease reference. Ways in which some producers do this is by splitting the video into modules (with headings), including a section index in the corner of the screen, or by using icons. For example, a training video on word-processing could be split into modules and subsections on the different functions and capabilities of the software, and then allocated numbers to help viewers home into specific functions or topics that they want to cover. A written index could also be provided with the video as a guide, showing the contents of the package.

Some traditional video producers are now looking at transferring their videos to CD-i or Video CD format. Both offer high-quality sound and images and, because they tend to be developed in a modular format, they offer the user more flexible access to the content. CD-i also has the capability to include more interactive elements (see pages 81–84).

Generic videos

Trainers have a wide choice of videos from publisher/ producers such as the BBC, Melrose, Sunday Times, Training Direct, and Video Arts. Video-based training packages are designed to help trainers learn to cope with different situations (such as group and individual sessions, or self-study), and offer effective presentations combining both the expert skills and knowledge of the trainer with the presentation of a high-quality video. Many packages are comprehensive, including a variety of aids: a main video presentation; a short video to reinforce the key learning-points; presenter guides (with hints on running training sessions or brainstorming); additional activities; participant guides; OHPs; and master handouts. Self-study workbooks and step-by-step plans for individual sessions may also form part of the package.

Customising a video

Most producers will customise a video if required, but this is likely to be costly. Customising can include anything from personalising the programme with a logo, cutting out inappropriate scenes, adding a message from the chief executive or a 'what-next' section at the end, to adding sequences and voice-overs.

Developing a bespoke product

Many companies team up with video producers to create productions for specific needs. Obviously there are many variables affecting the time and expense involved: your objectives, the format and style, and (not least) how much your budget will stretch to.

When you select a producer, ask what they have done before, and try to see some examples of their work. You should also have a clear idea from the start of what you want so that you can brief the producer intelligently. You should also think about how much personal involvement you want in the development of the video. One production company, Solent Video, said:

> Before a shoot it is essential that good research is carried out and that the customer and producer are looking in the same direction. In our experience, we find the more the client is involved in the production process, the better the end product will be. They are in the best position to pick out things that will not work: for example, someone smoking in a non-smoking area, an operator not wearing the right coloured overalls, etc. If using personalities, make sure that the person is not leaving the company shortly. All these things need to be considered to ensure the tape has as long a life as possible.

> The point is that any video needs to be informative, well put together, and meet the objectives. When deciding on the length of video, look for quality, *not* quantity – if you can tell your message in 15 minutes, do not take 20. As for developing a video, it is important that you catch and maintain the viewers' imagination within the first 30 seconds, so consider having a quick-fire, lively introduction. If they start fidgeting in their seats after two minutes, you have lost it and the approach is not working.

If you do wish to develop and produce a video, bear in mind these considerations:

∎ the objectives – what exactly are you trying to get across?

- your target audience – what is their present knowledge of the subject; what sort of thing is likely to appeal to them?
- the desired responses – what do you want the audience to think or do after watching the video?
- the format and style – do you want to use moving images, stills, presenters, drama?
- distribution – how will people get to see the video (individual viewing in the office or widescreen projection); will other materials be used with it; what sort of marketing and packaging will you need; and how many copies?
- timescale and budget – be very clear about how much time and money is available.

Once you have clarified all the above, you have to turn to the various phases of preproduction, production, and postproduction. In *preproduction* there are six stages:

Stage 1
The brief
This provides an overview of the video, its objectives, and background information on how you intend to show it to the target audience.

Stage 2
The outline
More detailed than the brief, this is a complete outline of the content: the information and ideas that you want to put across, and the key points to be made.

Stage 3
The treatment
At this point the producer will use the brief and outline to prepare a proposed 'treatment'. It will suggest techniques and styles to help get the messages across and so meet your objectives. Any support material may also be discussed at this stage.

Stage 4
The script
Once the treatment has been agreed, the producer then develops the script. This is the blueprint from which the director, camera crew, and editor work when shooting and

subsequently editing the video.

Stage 5

The storyboard Some productions will wish to develop the script into a storyboard (see Chapter 2).

Stage 6

Agreement of the final budget Once the script is complete, the producer will be able to provide you with a more accurate quotation for developing the video. If you agree with the script and costs, then the production process can start.

In *production* there are two stages:

Stage 1

Shooting the video The producer will use a professional crew to shoot the video, making best use of the resources and time available. At this stage he or she may ask you to view some 'rushes' (copies of the shots), help select shots for editing, and check their accuracy.

Stage 2

Developing support material If support material is to accompany the video, this will need to be commissioned now. Existing material within the company could be used, if appropriate.

The last phase is *postproduction*: once the individual sequences have been shot, they need to be assembled into a complete video. This is when the editing is done (according to the plan laid down in the script – stage 4 of preproduction). It is likely that the producer will show you the results at different stages to get your views and make any necessary adjustments.

In brief

■ There are many TBT formats - CD-ROM, CD-i, IV, Video CD, the Internet, satellite, and video-conferencing.

■ Some of the main strengths of multimedia are: ease of use and storage, the interactive element, learner control, flexibility, self-assessment facilities, feedback, and student-tracking systems.

■ TBT can be useful for training involved with: process, theory, keyboard skills, 'soft skills' (such as management skills, procedures, simulations, and product and service knowledge), and for refresher training.

■ To support multimedia you need a large storage capacity, a high-resolution colour screen, and data-processing capability to store, retrieve, and manipulate the data at high speeds and provide a responsive, flexible, and reliable system.

■ Authoring systems offer a high level of user-interaction. The systems on the market can take different approaches – a flow-line approach, or a page-based system.

■ There are four main options for developing TBT: to purchase generic materials, to personalise or to customise existing materials, and to develop a bespoke product.

■ Testing TBT materials is a continuous process. At the pilot stage a Beta version is usually produced so that the client can pilot it with potential learners.

■ When developing an audiocassette-based package you need to consider the introduction, access devices, tone of voice, script, how to maintain listeners' interest, and support material.

■ There are three main stages in developing a video: preproduction, production, and postproduction.

6 Materials for Group and Individual Learning

This chapter concentrates on developing some of the most commonly used activities for group and individual learning, such as materials for discussion exercises, role-plays, case-studies, business games and simulations, and portfolios.

Such face-to-face training covers many different interactions between people, such as group-based training and on-the-job training. When running this type of session you need to choose activities that:

■ enable learners to meet the training objectives

■ hold learners' interest.

If either ingredient is missing then the time and effort spent on the training will be wasted.

Type of activities

There are many types of exercise that can be used for group or individual learning sessions. They may be in the form of:

■ business games that can simulate 'real' situations. These are often used in learning that explores attitudes and behaviours, and develops skills in decision-making and problem-solving.

■ case-studies – a record of a 'real situation' that is given to participants to analyse and discuss. They can either be an illustration of a situation (eg how a company approached a specific problem), or a problem that might involve learners' analysing the situation and making their own decisions. Case-studies are often used in training sessions aimed at developing analytical thinking, and problem-solving/decision-making skills.

■ development plans – designed to enhance an individual's future effectiveness. It highlights the actions needed to improve performance.

■ discussion exercises – these involve changing attitudes, developing commitment, and exploring and sharing ideas and experiences.

■ learning diaries – for keeping a record of personal notes about learning experiences or incidents that individuals can review.

■ printed materials – handouts, check-lists, charts, questionnaires, quizzes, worksheets, and text-based open learning material (see Chapter 4)

■ portfolios – a means by which individuals can track and review their training development.

■ practical exercises – a simulation of a working situation, designed to confront learners with problems they might encounter in their actual job. Such exercises can help learners apply what they have learnt during the session (the theory) and summarise the main learning-points.

■ role-plays – providing opportunities to learn by 'doing'. Participants are presented with a situation that they have to resolve by acting out the roles of the people involved. Role-plays are often used for changing attitudes and developing personal skills.

■ work-based activities – using the work situation for learning purposes. They make use of learning opportunities that occur naturally in the workplace, and create opportunities to put learning into practice and thus aid further development.

Development options

Materials used in group or individual learning sessions will be affected by a number of factors such as those we have already discussed, eg the learning method selected, your objectives, the number of learners and their present knowledge, and the resources available.

There are three basic options when developing activities: to purchase generic, off-the-shelf materials, to adapt existing materials, or to develop a bespoke product. As for which option to make, the principles to guide you are explained in Chapter 4 (see pages 65 – 66) and Chapter 5 (see pages 94 – 96 and 105 – 107).

Generic materials

There is a wide choice of ready-made training materials (using a variety of media) for the busy trainer to tap into, covering many different skills and knowledge needs. Materials can be:

■ paper-based training courses or resource manuals. These include participative activities, role-plays, hand-outs, and OHTs, or any combination of these. Activities cover a wide range of skills, eg assertiveness, management, interpersonal skills, and developing team awareness.

■ video-based training packages. These make use of a combination of media: video, facilitator and participant guides, handouts, and OHTs. They offer trainers a complete resource which can be used whole or in part, depending on the learning situation.

■ business games. These include boardgames, computer games and simulations, and paper-based games.

Many of the materials mentioned above are relevant to any business, and can be used as they are, or adapted to meet your needs. Many come with photocopying licences and, if suitable, this option can save the designer both time and effort, releasing them to do other things. Why re-invent the wheel?

As for which activity to select, certain obvious criteria should be followed: choose activities that involve and excite participants, are relevant and realistic, are flexible, and provide clear briefs for participants and observers – and notes for the facilitator.

Adapt existing materials

If the designer finds that existing materials are weak in parts, it may be worth while adapting them. Some producers present their materials in a format that easily allows them to be customised. For example:

- Text-based PC training courses can be provided on disk or CD-ROM for in-house customisation: a cost-effective option if you are training large numbers of people.

- Some boardgames allow you to generate your own questions and answers on, for instance, company knowledge for induction courses, health and safety procedures or hazards, and new systems. When the questions have been designed, all you need to do is photocopy, or type, them onto blank cards for use in the game. This approach provides you with the flexibility to generate new questions for new situations.

- Why not consider customising activities by integrating personal issues that affect the participants? For instance, if managers have just taken responsibility for budgets within their departments, you could include questions that get them to consider monetary, as well as people, aspects of management within their own organisation, such as 'What budgetary constraints exist within your department?'

Bespoke products

In situations where no suitable resources exist, the only option is to develop something from scratch – a bespoke product. Although preparation can be time-consuming and (sometimes) costly, if you intend using the activity again on future occasions it need not turn out too expensive.

Developing activities

To be effective, activities must be carefully researched, planned, developed, tested, and the results measured. They should be easy to understand and use, and recreate the 'real' situation as closely as possible. They should also be challenging, intellectually stimulating, and contribute towards effective learning. Here we look at such activities as discussion groups, role-plays, case-studies, business games and simulations, individual learning, and portfolios. But first let us look at what goes into designing an activity.

Activity design considerations

As with the development of any materials, time spent on research and planning is always a sound investment. Figure 23, opposite, details the important factors that the designer should consider. (See also Figure 9, page 35.)

You may well want to add your own questions to those in Figure 23. By working through this fact-finding phase, I find it much easier to deal with the real issues and problems, and to focus on the desired outcomes.

Having identified the objectives, it then becomes necessary to design the learning process to help you meet them. The approach and the type of activity used will depend on your objectives. The experiential approach involves a series of processes that appeals to learners with different learning styles, thereby increasing the likelihood that something will be learnt. Activities can be used in different situations – role-plays for practising skills, or simulations to provide a structured learning experience.

The designer should consider:

■ setting time limits. Participants need to have boundaries within which to work. Allow time for briefing,

Figure 23

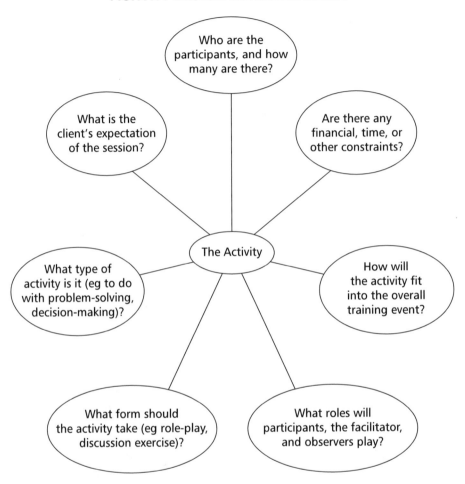

ACTIVITY DESIGN CONSIDERATIONS

undertaking the activity, and providing feedback.

■ a participant's brief. Each participant needs to know what is expected of him or her, and where help can be obtained.

■ guidelines for the facilitator. To help facilitators, the designer should provide adequate support information, thus enabling them to carry out their role effectively and get the most out of the activity, ie how to organise and run the activity, open and lead a discussion, de-brief, provide feedback, and summarise key learning-points.

▌ visual aids to assist groups in reporting back, eg flipcharts and OHTs (see Chapter 7).

Observer brief

Another important consideration at this stage concerns the observer, who plays an important role in many group activities. If you are designing an activity involving an observer, define first what his or her role is, keeping in mind that observers may be 'biassed' – they may stereotype people or may fail to retain an accurate record of the activity because of the amount of information involved. In other words, you should draw up a brief for the observer.

To avoid potential dangers, the observer should have a clear understanding of what is being assessed (eg behaviours, process skills) and be provided with a method for on-going recording (eg observation sheets – see below) during the session. This ensures that observations are made accurately.

The brief for the observer should ask him or her to define the type of contribution that each member of the group makes; individuals' personal styles; their behaviour towards others in the group (are they supportive; do they bring others into the discussion?); their skills; and their knowledge. Typically, such a brief includes information on who the participants are; details of the activity being undertaken and what is to be observed and assessed (eg behaviours, group interactions); and advice on how to record observations and provide feedback. Figure 24 shows an example.

Figure 24

OBSERVER BRIEF FOR AN ACTIVITY INVOLVING MEETING SKILLS

Your role is to observe what happens in a group meeting and report, as factually as you can, what you have seen. The aim is to provide helpful feedback to participants on how they performed both as a group and as individuals, so they can improve their performance.

During the session watch carefully and look out for the following points, recording your observations on the observation sheet (see below) provided:

▌ Do all members of the group understand the purpose of the meeting?

▌ How was the purpose clarified?

▌ Was good use made of the time available?

▌ Who contributed the most/least to the meeting?

▌ Did members of the group avoid issues that were difficult?

▌ Did they listen to one another?

▌ Were there any useful/unhelpful actions during this meeting?

▌ Any further comments.

On completion of the activity, summarise your findings under the headings given on the observation sheet, giving examples wherever possible (see Figure 25). Feedback can be given in the form of a group discussion on your observations. It should last about 30 minutes. During the discussion, comment on the strengths and weaknesses of the group, and those of each participant. You could also ask them for perceptions of their own behaviours and of how the group performed.

Observation sheets

The style and format of an observation sheet depends on the observer brief. To illustrate how such a sheet might look, I include an extract from one that I have used in the past for a course on staff development (Figure 25).

Imagine you are designing an observation sheet for a role-play that involves a manager carrying out a career-planning interview for a member of staff. The aim of the interview is to review the existing development plan, assess future potential against key factors, and draw up a new development plan to ensure that the potential is realised. (This exercise also provides learners with an opportunity to practise what they have already learnt.) During the role-play the observer needs to assess how the manager carries out the interview in terms of:

- the introduction – did they introduce the meeting by stating the objectives and agreeing an agenda?

- the discussion/drawing up a development plan – were all the points in the agenda covered? Was there two-way communication? How effectively did the manager assess future potential against the key factors provided? Did he or she consider a full range of development options? Was a development plan drawn up and agreed?

- the close – did the manager summarise what had been discussed and agreed? Did he or she gain commitment from the member of staff on further action (eg the development plan)?

- the manager's listening skills and questioning techniques – was it clear that he or she listened genuinely to the other person? What use did he or she make of open and probing questions? Did he or she summarise the discussion at various points in the conversation to check understanding?

At the end of the activity, the observer is asked to make suggestions on how the participants can improve their performance. To help keep a record of the activity an observation sheet (see Figure 25, opposite) should be included with the brief.

Discussion groups

The purpose of discussion groups is to get everyone contributing. How this is done depends on whether or not the group is to have a leader. This obviously affects the design of the activity. For example, in a leader-led discussion, guidelines should be provided to help the leader plan and ask questions that stimulate the discussion and so get participants involved. It is the leader's responsibility to help group members learn and to steer the group towards achieving the objectives. The essence of a leaderless discussion, however, is to give observers an opportunity to assess the performance of those involved against pre-determined criteria such as process skills or

Figure 25

OBSERVATION SHEET FOR A ROLE-PLAY

Observe the role-play closely and assess the performance of the participants, especially that of whoever is playing the manager, because this is the key role. Record your observations in the relevant boxes below as they occur, along with any suggested improvements in the way the participants could have handled the situation. If you think of any other matter in need of improvement but not listed here record it in the box at the bottom of the page. The role-play will take 15 minutes.

AREAS TO BE ASSESSED:	OBSERVATIONS/ COMMENTS	SUGGESTED IMPROVEMENTS
Introduction to the meeting		
The discussion and development plan		
The close		
COMMUNICATION SKILLS:		
Listening skills		
Questioning techniques		
OTHER AREAS NEEDING IMPROVEMENT		

personal styles. In this case, an observer brief is required.

Guidelines for the discussion leader may need to include suggested prompt questions to stimulate the discussion and bring out the main points, taking into account the objectives, the learners' background, and the time available. For example, prompt questions used in an exercise on customer relations might include:

■ What would you do if a customer started shouting at you?

▍ Whom would you ask if you could not solve that customer's problem?

▍ What impression would you want to give the customer?

▍ How would you give that impression?

Figure 26 provides an example of a participant's brief and Figure 27 shows a facilitator's guide for a discussion exercise, based on a video case-study on coaching. The facilitator's guide identifies for the leader the main points that should be brought out during the discussion after the exercise.

Figure 26

PARTICIPANT'S BRIEF

A coaching disaster

The video sequence you are about to see illustrates how not to coach someone (when compared with the recommended coaching practices we have discussed).

Watch the role-play between Jane and John. Then take five minutes to note how you think Jane went wrong, either in her approach or the words she used. Write down how you think she might have done things differently to achieve a more positive outcome.

What did she do wrong?	What could she have done differently?

When you have finished this exercise, discuss ideas as a group.

Figure 27

FACILITATOR'S GUIDE

What did she do wrong?	What could she have done differently?
She: ▮ left coaching too late ▮ criticised John in public ▮ made a personal attack on John ▮ focused on the negative rather than positive ▮ allowed no time for John's input ▮ became emotional.	She could have: ▮ arranged for coaching immediately after the event ▮ coached in private ▮ commented on the performance rather than the individual ▮ recognised good points ▮ involved John ▮ been supportive ▮ kept control of her emotions.

Role-plays

Role-plays are particularly useful for training that deals with attitudes and developing interpersonal skills such as assertiveness; interviewing techniques; communication skills; teambuilding; and behavioural change. Participants are asked to act out a situation that:

▮ requires them to acquire new skills best learnt by 'doing'

▮ encourages them to practise these skills in a non-threatening environment

▮ helps them to learn about themselves.

For example, in a staff appraisal course, where a manager is carrying out an appraisal of a member of staff, you might decide to use a role-play in which participants act out the role of the appraiser (the manager) and the appraisee (the member of staff being interviewed).

Design

Use the guidelines we discussed earlier in this chapter (page 114) to help you when you design your role-play. A few further points you might like to consider are:

▮ the number of people involved. I find that role-plays

in pairs or small groups of no more than four members tend to work the best. Remember, though, that the greater the number of people involved in a role-play the longer it takes to complete it.

∎ who will perform the role-plays. In many cases, they will be performed by the participants themselves, but there may be instances when there are advantages to using external people (eg professional actors) to act out some of the parts. For example, if you are using a role-play involving customer care skills, you may like to consider asking people from outside the organisation to play the role of the customer.

∎ how you will organise the role-plays. You could run them separately or simultaneously in pairs or groups, with or without an observer, and switching the roles around, so that all participants get a chance of practising the required skills. I have found that if you run role-plays simultaneously, people tend to feel less embarrassed and more likely to participate. Some people find acting in front of a group daunting.

Figure 28

EXAMPLE ROLE-PLAY – CUSTOMER CARE

Purpose	This activity is intended to give you the opportunity to develop your constructive questioning skills while dealing with a complaint from a customer. After the activity you will have the opportunity to receive feedback on your performance from the observer.
Approach	The scene is a building contractor's office. There are three roles: the receptionist, the customer, and the observer. Each participant will have an opportunity to play each of the roles. In terms of developing customer care skills, the key role is that of the receptionist. However, you may get insights and ideas on how you can improve your customer care skills from observing the others as well.
1	Each participant should identify a 'typical problem' that a customer may have if dealing with a building contractor (this

(continued opposite)

Figure 28 (cont)

EXAMPLE ROLE-PLAY – CUSTOMER CARE

		may be an actual problem you have dealt with, or an imaginary one). The problem should be used when you play the role of the customer. Do not reveal to the other participants the problem that you have selected.
	2	Form yourselves into groups of three. Decide in which order you are going to play the roles of receptionist, customer, and observer.
	3	Each role-play should take about 20 minutes to complete: 12 minutes for the role-play and eight minutes for the observer to provide feedback and discuss the participants' performance. Following feedback, change roles so that everyone in the group has an opportunity to practise the skills.
Roles		*Receptionist* You are a receptionist at a building contractor's office. Into reception comes a customer who is experiencing a problem with the service that your company is providing. You want to find out exactly what the problem is. Try to help the customer. Your first aim is to put the customer at ease, check what the exact problem is, and recommend what he or she should do.
		Customer The building contractor is carrying out some work for you but you are not happy with the service he is providing. You want to know what he is going to do to rectify the problem.
		Observer Your role is to observe the conversation between the receptionist and the customer, and to give some feedback to the participants on how they performed – especially the receptionist. Watch how the receptionist deals with the customer, how he or she attempts to identify the nature of the problem and attempts to solve it. Look for signs of passive listening, acknowledgement, and active listening. The following headings will help you to record your observations: ▪ How does the receptionist greet the customer? ▪ While the customer is complaining, how effectively does the receptionist keep silent? What acknowledgement signals are used to show that the receptionist is listening (eg nodding head, eye contact)?

(continued on page 124)

Figure 28 (cont)

EXAMPLE ROLE-PLAY – CUSTOMER CARE

Roles *(cont)*	▌ How effectively does the receptionist listen? ▌ Were the receptionist's questions clear? ▌ Any further comments?
	At the end of the role-play you will have an opportunity to give participants feedback. Summarise your findings and try to describe what you have seen, giving examples wherever possible.

Case-studies

Case-studies are in some ways similar to small group discussions and role-plays, but can also be structured as individual activities. They provide an opportunity for participants to apply what they have learnt by analysing the case-study. A typical one would involve a number of such tasks as:

▌ deciding what the problems are

▌ finding a solution

▌ finding mistakes in the case

▌ indicating how to do a procedure correctly.

The type of scenario you use is restricted only by the training objectives of the activity. Scenarios can be built around a conflict, a disciplinary matter, a financial affair, organisational systems and procedures, or the development of new products or a marketing and sales strategy. I often find examples from newspapers and magazines.

There are normally two parts to a case-study: the script for the trainer who will be administering it, and the study itself, which is distributed to the participants. The most common way of presenting case-studies is as written material, but they can also be presented in audio or video format.

Obviously, participants have to be given background information to the situation. For example, if participants are asked to develop a marketing strategy for a new product you could include fictional data from a market research survey, a company business plan, and sales statistics for competitors and for your own organisation. If any of the information you supply is factual rather than made up, you should of course change the names of those involved to protect confidentiality.

Business games and simulations

Business games and simulations come in a variety of formats: boardgames, building-models using Lego, paper-based or computerised games, or as something similar to the case-studies and role-plays we have just described.

They provide participants with opportunities to experience learning through personal involvement in a training event. They are active rather than passive, and offer an effective, fun, and creative way of developing skills and knowledge – they introduce a sense of playfulness in an otherwise sometimes stressful world. The exercises may have different contexts, but the underlying objective for all of them is to encourage 'experiential learning'. In this context, they provide an ideal opportunity for developing team spirit, an individual's strengths, or filling gaps in knowledge and expertise. More specifically, they can be used to emphasise particular concepts and techniques such as decision-making and problem-solving skills, allowing participants to make judgements and see the consequences in a risk-free environment. Another benefit is that participants gain insight, particularly during the debriefing, into their own behaviours as they react with others in the group.

Games and simulations provide, furthermore, opportunities to replicate other people's everyday work experiences. These are often unpredictable, so the designer simulates that reality by building randomness and change into the game. In group simulations, for instance, people may take on different roles (an operations manager might play the part of a director) in order to enact a range of realistic scenarios (eg running a strategic planning session). Such simulations can be especially helpful for training staff who work in a dangerous environment or with complex equipment.

A service company in the Midlands used a business game as part of a teambuilding course which focused on teamwork, planning, communications, decision-making, and leadership. Teams were asked to enact a true-to-life business scenario which drew on an unfamiliar environment. This involved completing a number of tasks, so participants had to work as a team and share their knowledge, skills, and expertise. On completion, there was an opportunity to analyse the results and what had been learnt in the game, to help participants relate this to their own jobs. The company found that the game showed participants how they personally dealt with similar issues in 'real' life, so providing them with a better understanding of what changes were necessary to improve their performance.

To take another example, a chemical company needed to train their technicians and electricians to use very expensive and complex processing equipment. There were insufficient numbers to run a cost-effective training course at any one time, and it was not feasible to let staff use the equipment immediately. The training solution that the company came up with was to develop a CBT simulation of the equipment. Staff started with the basics before gradually working up to more complex tasks and fault-finding, until they met the competencies required. One of the main benefits of using a simulation was that it reduced the risk of dangerous accidents and expensive mistakes on the actual equipment.

Developing a business game or simulation

How long does it take to develop a business game or simulation? This very much depends on what format you are using and the sophistication of the game. For example, if you are developing a role-play or practical exercise, it will clearly take less time than an interactive computerised simulation. Philip Sykes of Simulation Training describes how much the development time can vary:

> As a rule of thumb, an hour's classroom work requires 10 hours of development time. On the other hand, if we are developing a model-based simulation with lots of complex interactions between the decision and results, and where one outcome has an effect on another, this can take considerably longer. You may require 20, 30, or even 50 days of development work for one hour in the classroom. For example, one of our top-of-the-range business simulation exercises, 'Bissim' (an interactive, strategic, and financial simulation [see Figure 29]), took 1,000 hours to develop, and lasts 20 hours. This meant 50 hours of development for every hour's training.

Development usually involves two stages: the ideas stage, and the design stage. There is also the question of testing.

The ideas stage

In the first stage the designer sets behavioural objectives of the game or simulation, and explores ideas on how it should be developed. Typical objectives may be like those in Figure 29 on page 128 from 'Bissim', a business simulation exercise from Simulation Training.

Designers get the ideas they need from a variety of sources. In the past I have gathered them from brainstorming with colleagues, newspapers and magazine articles, TV game shows, and from looking at different approaches in training sessions.

Before I start the detailed design, I try out different ideas on colleagues in order to find out what works well. Useful feedback can also be gleaned from participants, and modifications then made to improve the design. If graphic designers and printers are likely to be needed I also discuss my requirements with them at this stage.

Figure 29

SETTING OBJECTIVES

'Bissim'
(Simulation Training)

The aim of this exercise is to help participants construct in their own minds a coherent picture or model of the nature of business and of the tasks of business management. More specifically, at the end of this exercise, they will be able to:

- explain the relationship between supply and demand in a market
- describe the effect of competition upon a business enterprise
- describe the relationship of investment, risk, and reward (or profit)
- describe the factors that contribute to and detract from teamwork and effective group process
- explain the process of collating and interpreting financial and market information.

If you are working with small groups, a boardgame or a game based on a case-study works well. For larger groups you could consider using a computerised business simulation that involves interaction between several groups, and can develop a competitive atmosphere.

Bridget Farrands of Team Talk partnership developed with her partner, Paul Clipson, a boardgame called 'Team Talk®' which takes an experiential approach to learning. Bridget explained how the idea for 'Team Talk' came about:

> It came out of one of our team development sessions for regional managers being run by Paul Clipson. He drew the outline of a race track on a piece of flipchart paper, rushed out to buy a set of dinky toy cars (to act as counters) and bars of chocolate (as prizes) and created a set of questions that dealt with issues the team were facing. The idea was that each person threw a dice, moved their car counter the appropriate number of spaces, and responded to a question. This

continued until everyone reached the 'finish' and the prizes were shared out.

The questions and the 'rules' were developed while the team participated in the game. We found that as they moved around the track, their readiness to disclose more about themselves, and what they wanted from each other during the game, led to questions that encouraged more risk. This in turn helped them to look at how they operated as a team, and what they wanted to do differently. The outcome of the game was never known at the start. We found that the familiar outline of the race track yielded dramatic results. In the three hours they played, the issues in the team were brought out, discussed, largely resolved, plans for future action were made, and a new mood of interest and commitment emerged.

The design stage

To be successful, a game must be genuinely useful, memorably enjoyable, and its message clearly conveyed. The design should also ensure that:

■ games have a clear and structured process

■ games allow individuals to have control over the actions and outcomes

■ the outcomes are not known at the start but evolve as the game is played

■ adequate information for facilitators is included to enable them to de-brief participants successfully.

In the design stage use is often made of case-studies, role-plays, and other techniques to create a real-life situation involving decisions, choices, and interactions. Many of the design considerations discussed earlier in this chapter are also relevant here.

You have to:

■ ensure that the format and type of game or simulation selected meets the needs. It is no use getting participants building with Lego if they do not *enjoy* building and manipulating things – they are unlikely to get much out of the exercise.

∎ be clear what is involved. An in-tray exercise aimed at helping supervisors manage their time may involve each participant working individually. The scenario is that they have returned from holiday and have to deal with a number of tasks that have arisen in their absence. They are asked to prioritise a list of tasks, deciding which they would delegate and which eliminate (a time limit for the exercise is set). At the end their decisions are reviewed.

∎ determine how the game is structured. In the case of a boardgame, you need to create a board with a pathway and decide how the participants will move around the board (using counters, dice, cards) and what each square will represent. What happens when a participant lands on a square? Will it direct the participant to another square, or ask him or her to pick up a card with a question on?

∎ decide what you will need to score and how. In a business simulation with participants running a business you may want to record (on paper or computer) the decisions they make, and score them with a rating system.

Testing

Testing happens continuously throughout the ideas and design stage.

Bridget Farrands found that, as 'Team Talk®' was developed, she and her partner:

> refined and improved the process in response to feedback from teams we worked with and our own observations. Part of the refinement of the game was to consider how we could use the structure so it did not offend significant groups, eg ethnic groups. This led to changing the race track (too male) into a circle

divided into sections, stopping the use of race cars, and making sure that the icons on the board were inclusive of as many groups as possible.

At the design stage you should test to discover whether a reasonable working design has been achieved. This may involve trying out your game or simulation on teams similar to your target audience – to show what people learnt from the experience, whether the objectives were met, and whether there was a change in performance or behaviour. Following a review of the feedback, the game can be modified: perhaps better questions are needed, or a simpler scoring system. This process continues until the designer feels confident that the game or simulation demonstrates improvements in performance and achieves the objectives. The following check-list should prove helpful here.

Check-list for testing games and simulations

- Was the game or simulation too complicated? It is, for instance, no use asking junior staff to analyse complex financial data if they have not had relevant training or experience. They will feel inadequate and be unable to participate fully in the exercise.

- In which situations did the game or simulation work best? Was it, say, when participants worked individually or in (small or large) groups?

- What particular advantages does your design offer? It might be that the game or simulation can be used for staff at different levels within the organisation, or that it stimulates discussion.

- Did the participants enjoy the experience?

- What turned out to be the key learning-points? In the case of a sales game, key messages may include 'Having the best product does not guarantee that you will get an order' or that 'Good communication within the company is important in providing good customer care.'

- Can the learners think of any improvements?

Individual learning

The two concepts of the learning organisation (the readiness and ability of an organisation to learn from its collective experience) and individual learning on a continuing basis have gained much ground in recent years. Flatter organisational structures now mean fewer opportunities for promotion, so people are looking at new ways to keep up to date and to broaden their knowledge and skills. Learners can do a lot on their own, but they should not be left solely to their own devices. Many people need some form of support, feedback, and encouragement. There may be occasions, for instance, when one-to-one training is provided on the job or for self-development. In these situations you need to design your learning sessions and materials for a particular individual rather than a group of people.

The same principles of designing learning materials apply whether you are designing them for an individual or a group: the objective is to improve performance: this can be related to people's knowledge, skills, and aspirations. This is paramount, and can be achieved by using such techniques as coaching, instruction, providing opportunities for practice, working with colleagues, and discussions. (See also another title in this series, *Cultivating Self-development*, by David Megginson and Vivien Whitaker, IPD, 1996.) Here we look at personal development (or 'action') plans, work-based learning activities, learning diaries, and portfolios ('learning logs').

Personal development plans

To help individuals manage their learning it is useful to draw up a personal development plan with their manager, coach, or mentor (see Figure 30). This typically includes:

- what learners need to practise or follow up
- how to do so, and when
- specific action steps they must take, and by what date
- any additional issues or concerns they need to address.

Figure 30

PERSONAL DEVELOPMENT PLAN

Proposed action to improve job performance	Planned completion date	Person responsible for initiating training

Work-based learning activities

Many companies now encourage managers to use work itself as a medium for learning and development – the aim being to help learners transfer new knowledge and skills to their own workplace. In other words, there is now a great stress on *work-based* learning activities, which allow individuals some degree of control over what, how, and when they study. To help people transfer new learning to their own situations, activities should refer to their individual experiences – and it is surprising how many learning opportunities can be created in this way.

Remember, if you are designing a work-based activity, to take into account any support or formal training the learner may need.

Example of a work-based activity

Practise writing a draft report using the company guidelines on 'Report-writing'. Discuss the result with your manager and ask for feedback to identify your strengths and also the areas that can be improved upon. Agree further action.

Learning diaries

Learning diaries are personal notes kept so that learners can analyse and draw lessons from their experiences during the working day. Typically they include a brief description of the learning situation, details on what was learnt from it, and any action to be taken. (An example of a learning diary is set out in Figure 31.) Because they usually end up holding quite a bit of information, it may be worth considering a landscape design to provide yourself with more room to write in.

Figure 31

LEARNING DIARY FORMAT

Date	Activity/experience	Learning points	Further action needed

Portfolios (learning logs)

It is now generally acknowledged that learning (education and training) is a continuing process and may take many forms, and not necessarily just those of conventional types of training. With the rapid pace of change (whether technological, social, political, or scientific), there is a growing need for us to go on developing our skills and knowledge after initial professional and occupational training – to keep up to date and competent.

Portfolios (sometimes otherwise referred to as learning logs) are one device to help us keep abreast:

▌ for professional development
▌ self-development
▌ as a basis for discussion with managers, mentors, or coaches
▌ to help review progress towards a development plan, and to update it as needed
▌ as an integral part of a training programme leading to an NVQ (eg as the basis of discussion with an NVQ assessor)

▌ for job interviews

▌ as part of an assessment centre

▌ as a basis for staff appraisal and career- or succession-planning.

A portfolio is essentially a structured way of recording our personal learning experiences and achievements. It can help individuals review an experience, draw conclusions from it, and plan further action.

Designing a portfolio (learning log)

Constructing and compiling a portfolio is a learner-centred experience. It involves learners in a process of self-evaluation, reflection, and action-planning. There is no right or wrong way to develop a portfolio; but it should be adapted to suit an individual's style and needs, and include all the relevant sections (eg those covering formal and informal learning). Portfolios normally consist of three parts:

Part 1   for official documents (qualifications, certificates, and diplomas)

Part 2   for your personal development plan (or 'learning contract')

Part 3   for notes about learning experiences – a bit like a personal diary.

You may however want also to consider providing evidence through other media such as audio and video (eg the delivery of a training or coaching session).

As a trainer, you may want to provide individuals with some guidelines and thought on how to set up and keep a portfolio. For example, you could work with learners to carry out a skills-competence audit, so that they can reflect on the past before setting future goals.

The starting-point when designing a portfolio is to be clear *why* you are constructing one, and to be able to answer the following questions:

- Where am I now – in terms of skills, competencies, and achievements?
- Where am I heading – in terms of goals and aspirations?
- What do I need for the journey – in terms of the skills, knowledge, or experience for achieving my goals?

Answering these questions helps individuals draw up a personal development plan which can form the basis of a portfolio. Evidence of all sorts can then be gathered: reports, an extended CV, evaluations of training events, testimonials, course brochures, certificates, and qualifications.

In brief

- There are a wide variety of activities for group and individual learning: discussion exercises, role-plays, case-studies, games, simulations, work-based activities, and portfolios.
- Some key considerations when designing activities are: the objectives; what is expected of the participants; the number of learners; the duration of the activity; equipment requirements; and the role of participants, the observer, and the facilitator.
- Activities should have clear objectives, a set time-limit, a clear brief for participants, and guidelines for the observer and the facilitator.

Visual Aids

Training sessions can be much enhanced by the use of visual aids. To be successful, though, they need to be relevant, well-produced, easy to understand, and introduced at the appropriate point in the session. In this chapter I discuss a variety of materials that can be used to create interest, motivate learners, and help people to understand and recall information.

Designing visual aids

Any visual aid must be carefully designed or, if existing materials are being used, checked to ensure that it meets your objectives.

Design considerations

The prime objective of visual aids is to make the message clear (in that regard, many of the guidelines we discussed in Chapters 1 to 3 also apply here). The questions that you need to consider from a design point of view are these:

■ Will a given visual aid meet your requirements: does it contain all the information that you want to put across? Is it clear? If the information is complicated, consider building it up step by step – for example, by using several transparencies to lay over a basic overhead transparency (OHT).

■ At which point in the training session will the visual aid be used? Decide whether you should gradually show part, or all, of it – and when. Think also about how much time it is likely to take you to discuss the aid, and the time required for taking and answering questions.

Basic design rules

∎ Keep the information clear, simple, and readable.

∎ Check that people can see the aid clearly.

∎ Use colour to add interest and to highlight key points.

∎ Position the different components eg on an OHT in such a way that viewers are not confused by them; the design should ensure a balance relative to the purpose.

∎ Avoid elaborate tables, figures, charts, and diagrams – they may distract viewers.

∎ To highlight information draw a circle around the figures or data that you want people to focus on.

∎ Think about the maximum distance that viewers will be from the screen, flipchart, or whiteboard, so that you can determine what size of lettering is needed (see below).

Briefing the producer

Whether the producer is in- or out-of-house, you should include in the brief:

∎ the date by which the material must be ready

∎ details of the type of visual aid(s) required

∎ the objectives

∎ the size of the room and screen (if applicable) – this will determine the size of lettering

∎ the budget.

Preparation

No matter how well your visual aids are produced, if you do not have efficient equipment, or do not present them well, they will not meet your objectives. The aids are only as good as their presentation, so think carefully about the following points.

When selecting the type of equipment that you want for your chosen visual aid, consider its:

∎ practicality
∎ durability
∎ ability to assist the audience's understanding of the subject
∎ cost (if purchased, would it prove a good investment, or should you hire it?)
∎ portability
∎ availability.

Types of visual aid
Flipcharts

Easy to use and inexpensive, these are ideal for small groups and can be prepared in advance. They are often used for: stimulating interaction between learners and facilitator; brainstorming; writing up session objectives or instructions; recording and reviewing key points from learners; and responding to queries. Sheets from flipcharts can also be displayed like posters following discussion.

Using flipcharts

Flipcharts can be used flexibly, with pages prepared in advance or created during the session by you or the learners (eg to record ideas or results). Preparing your flipchart materials in advance saves time and effort during the session; also, the flipcharts may conveniently be used as *aides-mémoire* of key messages. Ensure that you:

∎ make information concise and readable
∎ keep your points to the minimum – the key messages
∎ use large letters (about two to three inches high) so that the information stands out

■ use coloured pens for variety and easier reading (but avoid pale colours such as yellow, which can be difficult to read)

■ write on every other page to avoid 'show-through' of the ink and to keep an element of surprise about what is to come

■ put tabs on the side of each sheet (which also helps you to turn the pages), or number them to keep them in sequence, so that you can find topics quickly

■ put notes to yourself on the flip in light pencil to aid you during the presentation.

Whiteboards

Whiteboards have a glossy finish that is easy to clean, and are normally wall-mounted or else come with a stand. Some have a magnetic back (useful for putting up additional learning aids – eg ones made out of card), and a photocopier to print off an image on the board.

Overhead transparencies (OHTs)

Easy to store and reuse, OHTs are a popular visual aid for many trainers, particularly for larger, more structured group sessions. Transparencies are either prepared or used blank during a training session (eg so that the trainer may illustrate further points).

Using OHTs

OHTs are useful if you want to:

■ show the development of an idea

■ illustrate key points

■ describe quickly and clearly things not easily expressed in words (eg statistics)

■ collect participants' ideas.

There are a number of practical considerations that you should address:

▪ Decide on a clear design, making sure all the OHTs are obviously part of the same series used in the session.

▪ Decide which OHTs you want to present as finished product and which you want to add to during the session (eg with learners' feedback after a problem-solving exercise).

▪ Make sure that each OHT expresses one idea only; include no more than, say, six lines of text.

▪ Use large lettering and check legibility from a distance: as a rule of thumb, one-inch lettering is visible up to 30 feet away, two-inch at 60 feet.

▪ Make the blank space between lines about one and a half times the letter height.

▪ Restrict bullet lists to no more than four points.

▪ Avoid printed or typewritten documents, tables, and forms. These will probably be too small and therefore difficult to read.

There are various materials that you need:

▪ *specialised pens*. With water-soluble ink, images can easily be removed using a damp cloth; in the case of permanent ink, the only way to remove images is by using spirit.

▪ *transparency film*. This can come in individual A4 sheets or as a roll of acetate. Light-weight film (0.8mm thickness) is good for single use, but for multiple use go for 1.2mm. Film is also available ready-printed (eg with graphs).

▪ *design cards*. These can simplify transparency-making (eg for positioning and setting out your content) and come in lined or grid form.

▪ *equipment*. A thermal copier or photocopier can be used (each needs film with a specially treated surface) to copy text or illustrations onto the overhead transparency. To produce OHTs on computer you need dedicated software with graphic facilities and a laser printer.

▮ *mounts*. OHTs can be presented mounted onto rigid frames, attached with tape, or inserted into clear pre-punched pockets with two flaps that fold outwards (this is useful for storing the OHTs in a file).

Other tools for developing OHTs are a compass, rule, transfers (ie of letters), and transparent coloured foils which you cut to shape and stick onto your film.

To make effective use of your OHTs, it is important to prepare before the training session. A check-list that I use to help me do this is set out below.

Pre-session check-list

1. Check that OHTs are in order and the right way up.
2. Check that the appropriate equipment is working.
3. Make sure that there is a spare lightbulb.
4. Check that the plate and lens (or computer screen) are clean.
5. Check the distance between screen and viewers.
6. Try out an OHT and focus the image so that it fills the screen.
7. If you have to use a wall rather than a screen, make sure that the image is not projected onto the corners or onto curtains.

When actually using the projector, follow these tips:

▮ Place your transparency on the projector before switching on.
▮ Make sure that each OHT is aligned properly on the screen.
▮ Cover up longer texts with some card or a piece of paper, and uncover one point at a time.
▮ Point to things on the OHT itself, not the screen.
▮ Do not leave an OHT on once you have finished with it – it will compete for attention with what you are saying.
▮ Make sure that you do not obstruct anyone's view.

Slides and electronic presentations

Traditionally slides were 35mm and produced by specialist firms. With the introduction of new technology, though, slides and computer-generated presentations can be easily produced using a PC. Electronic presentations are being used more and more by companies to deliver training because they provide creative ways to present materials. By linking up a computer or video recorder with a monitor or projector, high-quality presentations can be generated on screen. With today's graphic presentation software, such as Microsoft Powerpoint and Lotus Freelance, the trainer now has the facilities to develop professional materials quickly and at little cost. These packages allow you to include text, graphics, and colour in your OHTs and slides. One of the main advantages, furthermore, of producing images on computer is that they can be easily updated, rearranged, and reproduced.

Using slides and electronic presentations

Be aware of all the possibilities open to you:

■ Make use of a wide variety of data and images – eg spreadsheets and graphics – from other software which can be imported (transferred) into your presentation.

■ Use photographs of situations not normally accessible (eg health and safety hazards).

■ Use a scanner to incorporate other documents and photographs.

■ Think about incorporating elements of an existing in-house video into your presentation.

■ Use the OHTs as handouts. This reduces note-taking during sessions. For example, the computer can be used to reduce the size of OHTs or slides so that two or three images can be fitted in down the left-hand side of the page, leaving space on the right for notes.

Whatever you decide to use, bear in mind that visual aids should:

- reinforce key learning-points
- help to summarise and organise information, and act as a point of reference for the audience (eg good handouts reduce the need for writing notes during the course)
- be clear and understandable so that learners can easily relate to them.

Other considerations include: the audience, the objectives, and the type of training in question; the subject matter; what will increase participants' interest and motivation to learn; and what visual aids are the ones that you personally feel comfortable with. There may also be practical constraints such as cost, resources, and time. For instance, should your organisation have the internal expertise to produce the materials you require, then costs will be reduced; but could the time be spent better on doing something else – like delivering more training? You have to weigh up the cost benefits of each option. And will the materials be cost-effective – how often are they likely to be used?

Before you decide to develop materials from scratch, carry out some research into what is available. Consider all the options: to use existing materials as they are; to adapt them; or to develop a bespoke product. Common ways of adapting materials include:

- updating them – eg to meet current legislation, or to describe new procedures and policies
- improving the design and layout as a result of feedback
- adapting the language – changing the tone and style to suit different audiences
- changing the format – using, say, part of a handout as an OHT.

In brief

▮ Visual aids come in many forms – flipcharts, OHTs, slides, and computer-generated presentations.

▮ They are best used to illustrate key facts.

▮ The information should be clear, simple, and readable.

▮ Pay attention to detail – eg page layout and the size and style of typeface.

References

BOYDELL T and LEARY M *Identifying Training Needs.* London, IPD, 1996.

BRAMLEY P *Evaluating Training.* London, IPD, 1996.

Continuing Professional Development, IPD (to be published 1996)

COTTON J *The Theory of Learning.* London, Kogan Page, 1995.

DEAN C and WHITLOCK P *A Handbook of Computer-based Training.* Third edn, London, Kogan Page, 1992.

Dworkin G and TAYLOR R *The Copyright, Designs and Patent Act 1988.* London, Blackstone Press, 1994.

ELGOOD C *Handbook of Management Games.* Fifth edn, London, Gower, 1993.

GREEN P *Quality Control for Print Buyers.* London, Blueprint, 1992.

HARDINGHAM A *Designing Training.* London, IPD, 1996.

HONEY P and MUMFORD A *The Manual of Learning Styles.* Third edition, Honey, 1992.

LOWE R *Successful Instructional Diagrams.* London, Kogan Page, 1994.

MEGGINSON D and WHITAKER V *Cultivating Self-development.* London, IPD, 1996.

PARKER R *Looking Good In Print*. Third edn, London, Ventana Press, 1993.

RAE L *Measure Training Effectiveness*. Second edn, London, Gower, 1992.

REAY D *Understanding How People Learn*. London, Kogan Page, 1994.

ROWNTREE D *Preparing Materials for Open, Distance and Flexible Learning*. London, Kogan Page, 1994.

STIMSON N *How To Write and Prepare Training Materials*. London, Kogan Page, 1994.

I Index

access devices
  audiocassettes 102
  open learning packages 68
  videos 104–5
action plans, for open learners 74–5
activities 34–6, 83, 110–36
  for open learners 69–72, 74
  see also work-based activities
aims 12
  see also objectives
alignment of text 47
animation 50, 79
artificial intelligence 80
assignments, in open learning 72–3
audiocassettes 61, 101–3
audiovisuals 101–8
authoring systems 92–4

bespoke training materials 17, 18–19, 113–14
  open learning packages 66
  TBT packages 96
  videos 106
Bissim (simulation exercise) 127, 128
boardgames 113, 125, 128–9, 130
bold type 47
borders, graphic design 44, 48
boxes, graphic design 44, 48–9
budgets 16, 66–7, 93–4, 107, 108
bullet points 44, 48, 141

business games 110, 112, 113, 125–31

case-studies, use of 67, 110–11, 124–5
CBT (computer-based training) 80–81, 89
  quality standards 28
  student-tracking systems 39, 40
  use in open learning 61
CD-i 61–2, 81–4, 90, 92
CD-ROM 81–4
  costs 16
  equipment 90–91, 92
  student-tracking systems 39, 84
  use in open learning 61–2
clip art 50, 79
colours, use of 44, 51–4, 138
commitment to training, need to gain 5–6, 17
compact discs *see* CD-i; CD-ROM; video CD
competencies 6–7, 8
computer-based training *see* CBT
computer-generated presentations 143
content of learning materials 13–14, 31–6
copyright 16, 19–21, 95
costs 16

of authoring systems 94
of developing open learning
    packages 66–7
of TBT 94–5
of using colours 52, 53
customised training materials 17, 18,
    113, 144
    open learning packages 65
    TBT packages 95–6
    videos 105

decorative typefaces 46
design considerations and processes 1,
    5–19, 23–36
    activities 114–16
    business games 129–130
    portfolios 135–6
    role-plays 121–2
    TBT packages 97–101
    text-based open learning
        materials 67–75
    visual aids 137–9
    see also graphic design
design specifications 1, 5–19
development plans see personal
    development plans
diagrams, use of 50, 79, 138
discussion exercises 111, 118–21
'drop shadow' boxes 48–9

electronic presentations 143
equipment
    for TBT 81–2, 90–92
    for visual aids 138–9, 141
evaluation of training 37–40
experiential learning 1–2, 114, 125, 128
expert systems 80

facilitators 115–16, 120–21, 129
feedback 4, 34–6, 37, 38, 39, 89
    facilities of CD packages 83
    in CBT 80

in open learning 69–70
role of observers 116–17
use of video 104
flipcharts 139–40
flowcharts, use in TBT design 93, 99
footers 49
formats
    computer screens 100
    open learning materials 60–63
    printed learning materials 42–4
    TBT 79–87
framework for material
    development 4
functional specifications 30, 99–100

games see business games
generic training materials 17, 18,
    112–13
    CD packages 81
    interactive video systems 84
    open learning packages 65
    TBT packages 94–5
    videos 105, 112
graphic design 42–54
graphics, use of 50–51, 79
graphs, use of 44, 50–51

handouts 47, 143, 144
hardware for TBT 81, 82, 90–92
headers 49
hotspots 98–9

icons 49–50, 68, 93, 104
identification of learning needs 5–6
illustrations, use of 43, 50–51
    see also diagrams; graphs;
        photographs
in-tray exercises 130
indentation of text 48
instructional design 97
interactive
    multimedia, definition of 76–9

video *see* IV
   writing 33–4
Internet 62–3, 85–6
introductions to learning
      materials 36, 68–9, 98
italic type 46–7
IV (interactive video) 61–2, 84–5
   see also video

justified text 47

keyboard skills, use of TBT in training
      for 88

language courses 102, 103
layouts 45
learners
   profiles and characteristics of 7–11
   support for 17, 38, 63–4, 85
learning
   activities *see* activities
   cycle 1–2
   diaries 74, 111, 133–4
   environment 16, 17
   logs 134–6
   models 27
   needs, identification of 5–6
   objectives 12–13, 14, 127, 128
   styles 2–3
lettering *see* typefaces; typesize;
      typestyles
logos 49, 79

monitoring materials 37–40
MPEG cards 91, 92
multimedia 76–9
   equipment for 90–92

NVQs (national vocational
      qualifications) 7, 27, 69, 134

objectives 6, 7, 12–13, 14, 127, 128

observation sheets 117–18, 119
observer briefs 116–17, 123–4
'off the shelf' materials *see* generic
      training materials
OHTs *see* overhead transparencies
open learning 57–75
outline plans 11–17
overhead transparencies (OHTs) 45,
      46, 54, 140–42, 143

Pantone Matching System (PMS) 53
paper, for printed learning
      materials 55–6
paragraphs 44, 48
participants' briefs 115, 120
performance standards 6–7, 12
personal development plans 111,
      117–18, 132–3, 134, 135, 136
personalised training packages *see*
      customised training materials
photographs, use of 43, 50, 79
pie charts, use of 51
piloting materials 37, 38, 101
PMS *see* Pantone Matching System
portfolios 111, 134–6
printers, relations with 54–5
product knowledge, use of TBT 89
project plans 23–6, 68

quality criteria, selection of
      materials 19, 20
quality standards 26–7, 28, 38
questionnaires 38–9, 65, 74, 83

readability of materials 29, 33–4, 45,
      48
retention levels 77
reviews with learners 39, 74
role-plays 83, 88, 102, 104, 111,
      121–4
   observer's role in 117–18, 119
roman type 46–7

routing systems 99

sans serif typefaces 45–6
satellite training 86–7
screen formats 100
script typefaces 46
selection
  of learning materials 17–19
  of training methods 15
self-assessment 65, 83
serif typefaces 45–6
session plans 30
simulations 83, 88–9, 110, 111,
  125–31
size of lettering *see* typesize
slides 45, 46, 47, 54, 143
sources of learning materials 17–19
  CD packages 81
  open learning packages 65
  TBT packages 94–5
  videos 105
spacing of text 44, 48, 141
standards
  for multimedia hardware 91, 92
  of performance 6–7, 11, 12
  of quality 26–7, 28, 38
storyboarding 30–31, 99, 108
student-tracking systems 39, 40, 84
study plans 73
support for learners 17, 38, 63–4, 85
SWOT analysis 25

TBT (technology-based training) 15,
  76–109
  copyright 21, 95
  costs 16, 94–5
  functional specifications 30,
    99–100
  introductions to packages 36, 98
  use of icons 49–50, 93, 104
  see also CBT; CD-i; CD-ROM; IV;
    Internet; satellite training

Team Talk (boardgame) 128–9,
  130–31
testing
  learners 10, 70, 90, 95, 98
  materials 37–40, 101, 130–31
text-based open learning materials 62,
  64–75
time-scales
  for development of materials 15,
    66, 126–7
  for training 14
tints, graphic design 44, 49, 53–4
titles of learning materials 36
training
  evaluation of 37–40
  methods, selection of 15
  needs, identification of 5–6
  specifications *see* design
    specifications
transparencies *see* overhead
  transparencies; slides
typefaces 44, 45–7
typesize 43, 44, 47, 138, 141
typestyles 44, 46–7

video 79, 103–8
  see also IV
video CD 85
video-conferencing 63, 85, 87
visual aids 137–45

white space 43, 47, 48
whiteboards 140
wording
  of learning materials 29, 33–4
  of objectives 13, 14
work-based activities 15, 39, 111,
  133
writing
  learning materials 33–6
  objectives 13, 14